Cutting Expenses & Getting More for Less

Cutting Expenses & Getting More for Less

◆

41+ Ways to Earn an Income from Opportune Living

Anne Hart

ASJA Press

New York Lincoln Shanghai

Cutting Expenses & Getting More for Less
41+ Ways to Earn an Income from Opportune Living

Copyright © 2005 by Anne Hart

ASJA Press
an imprint of iUniverse, Inc.

iUniverse books may be ordered through booksellers or by contacting:

iUniverse
2021 Pine Lake Road, Suite 100
Lincoln, NE 68512
www.iuniverse.com
1-800-Authors (1-800-288-4677)

ISBN: 0-595-34772-X

Printed in the United States of America

Contents

1

Live on Less for a Living

Getting more for less attracts buyers. You get what you pay for. Here are practical steps for all ages in this guide to healthier, lower cost hunting in hidden markets. Pay less using high-quality, highly focused comparison shopping. If you want to make a living sharing the practical applications of living on less or getting what you pay for, high-quality bargain hunting, or home-made product tips, your idea *must have redemptive value for a universal audience.* Show others how to have fewer expenses, higher quality, and more benefits by comparison shopping in the hidden markets, watching evolving trends, and making use of information so new that the consumer media and industrial trade journals haven't seen it yet. Or, live the frugal lifestyle yourself.

Look for a way to improve the quality of whatever you buy with fewer unnecessary expenses. You need a monthly budget, a plan, and access to new information. You find this information by going where vendors go to buy or sell surplus and attending the free exhibit halls of trade shows where you can talk to vendors and suppliers, wholesalers, and re-sellers.

Begin by looking for surplus, shelf-pulls, and overstocked items. Live on less yourself, and enjoy the comfort. Or make a living by teaching others how to live on less. Check out comparison shopping Web sites such as Nex Tag at: http://www.nextag.com/ or other sites. Use the keyword: comparison shopping on your computer search engine, for example: http://www.google.com. If you type in "comparison shopping" what comes up are numerous Web sites for price comparison. Share information on how to live on less. You can earn a living by showing others how to live on less. And you can live on less and save the rest for a time when you'll be mature enough to really appreciate having experienced the creativity of expanding your skills.

When you measure and budget time as well as money, you can record and share how and why you live on less. When you need more money, start a home-based business showing people how to live on less. This can be done online, in print, or by putting on living on less conferences or meetings. You can start a national or local chapter of a living on less special interest group.

Living on less can be part of a personal, oral, or family history business recording life stories with a new slant. What did people do to live on less? How can you live on less today and still enjoy comfort, less frustration, and more free time for play—and at the same time make sure you never outlive your savings or are left destitute in your old age? There are ways to play and enjoy living on less while making more money.

The formula is to show how other people lived on less and enjoyed saving. Your objective is to give information, techniques, strategies, tips, and solutions to problems that get clear, tangible and immediate results.

What are some techniques for living on less? How can you use what's already around your house in order to enjoy creative play at home and live comfortably on less—less stress, less income, and less clutter? Do only what is simple and clear to understand.

You need to live on less in a hurry. Around your home you see two phones, and a computer with a recording drive capable of saving files to a CD or DVD. Quick, how do you generate money at home with what you have around the house? You can try out software for a month for a free trial. You can even set up a free Web site. Your first step would be to run an inexpensive audio cable from your telephone to your computer.

Next would be to acquire or try out software that records the human voice or any sound from your phone into your computer. Start with the software Total Recorder. See the High Criteria's Web site at: http://www.highcriteria.com/. It's inexpensive and handy for recording the human voice or any sound. There's also Phone-In Buddy. See http://www.transcriptionbuddy.com/PB_main.htm. You can try a free trial of various types of software. Or you can try other dictation software, which also allows anyone to call you, talk in your phone, and have their voice and yours (or their voice alone if you don't speak) recorded into your computer as an audio file. Dictran is another company offering various types of dictation software. See http://www.theprogrammers.com/dictran.html.

You could attach a $10 computer microphone to your computer to record your own voice into your computer. Or for recording either your voice or someone else's voice that makes a call to your telephone, you'd use a $2 or $3 telephone pick up device attached to your phone and to a tape recorder.

Then whatever is saved on the tape recorder (or digital recorder) can be saved in your computer. With old fashioned tape recorders, you'd need an audio cable connecting your tape recorder to your computer while you use software such as Total Recorder to record what's on the tape to your computer.

Alternatively, use the newer digital tape recorders that allow you to plug them into your computer and save what's recorded to your hard drive. The point is that you save whatever people say on the phone from your computer to a CD or DVD.

The way you make money is to let people tell significant events in their life stories. They can talk about what they did at any stages of their lives. Or they can dictate love letters to a spouse for an anniversary present, or talk about plans, wills, testaments, events at various life stages, messages to relatives to be saved for future generations as a time capsule.

They can record anything legal when they telephone you. They can even mail you audio tapes. What you do is save all these audio recordings on a CD or DVD and mail it back to them for a fee—$10 to $25.

If you know how to scan a photo or save a video clip, you can quickly learn how to save the photo or video clip to the same CD or DVD along with their voice and the transcribed voice as text. That way, the text gets printed out on paper and put in a pretty folder in case relatives in the far future want to know what is on the disk but can't play it. You have a time capsule. That's one way to generate money fast using what's around your home and helping people share memories and life stories.

These specific strategies, examples, and techniques for living on less are divided into age groups. How to live on less at 18 or 28 would be quite different from how to live on $500 a month at 65 or at 85. Living on less with children is different from living on less as an empty nester in late middle age. Whatever your stage of life, there are specific strategies you can use to live on less and still live comfortably. If you want to work at home online, there are strategies for finding income.

Living on less is available to those with book learning or street intelligence gained from experience. It's a matter of using less processed foods and finding new housing alternatives. For those with children, home schooling and neighborhood-based education are two alternatives. Nutritious foods for less don't have to be starchy or sweet fillers. You can grow certain herbs and vegetables in window sill planters or community gardens within urban areas, even if you don't have a backyard or live in an efficiency apartment.

In these seventeen chapters, consider the practical applications of how to live on less. It's a matter of learning what you need, how to find it, and why you need it. You'll also need to know whom to contact, when, and where to locate what you require to live on less.

Quality depends on the basic materials. To live on less and have the quality of life you require for health, start with basic, unprocessed foods, clothing, and shelter. To earn an income without working for someone else or without investing huge amounts of money in a business, you need basic equipment. This equipment would be an industrial-quality camcorder, a computer with fast Internet access, and a laser printer.

When you pare down to bare bones what you need to live on less, what you need to survive at home is a computer with Internet access in order to earn money at home. With fast Internet access for generating income, you don't need a car, car insurance, or any other expense, such as gasoline costs to generate income.

If you already own a car that's in good shape, you can use it as an online and a mobile workplace for extreme telecommuting. Work online from your moving vehicle and travel the world wireless. If you use the bus to move around your area, don't buy a car when you can buy a house for the same initial investment.

As a practical example, I live on less as a retired (former) part-time university educator in creative writing. My income is $500 a month plus freelance writing income. Royalties from my books average about $800-$900 a year. Income from freelance writing averages about $300 a year from magazines. I could write more freelance articles to increase my income. In the past, through eBay, I sold everything in my house that I did not use, which netted me $2,000. You can sell on eBay for a living. Or sell from your own Web site if you offer a service that attracts high traffic.

You can create online courses. If there's a need for a course online in my field of experience, I teach it online as an independent contractor. My fields include creative writing, personal history, and genealogy. I'll work in any field that someone with a general liberal arts education can comfortably handle. These fields include journalist and personal history, genealogy, and creative writing.

When I need quick money, I take my camcorder, record people's personal histories—significant life events and turning points—on DVDs or CDs. I give my clients copies of the disk, tape, DVD, or CD. They put the material into a time capsule, family prayer box, or scrap book. If clients want, I'll upload their life stories on tapes, CDs, or DVDs to their purchased Web sites. I use Microsoft Front Page to upload to their Web sites life stories on digital video disks or CDs.

To generate income, collect quotes from the rich and famous. Obtain permission to put the comments into an article, book, pamphlet, or booklet. Copyright your compilation of quotes in your name. Then compile these comments into a book or pamphlet with the byline, "edited by——your name." Questions many tabloids ask celebrities include "What's your favorite original recipes?" Instead, ask powerful people, "What's the most important lesson you learned from life?"

Write to people you admire. Did you ever think of writing letters to 2,000 famous people asking this question, "What is the most important lesson you learned from life?" What if almost all the celebrities, physicians, billionaires, scientists, or famous authors replied with common sense advice such as, "Make the most of what you have?" You could put this title on your book, pamphlet, booklet, or article. Put their voices on a DVD or CD with the answer to that interview question.

This is what marketing simplicity and commitment is all about—*making the most of what you already have*. It sells because it appeals to almost all people everywhere. The secret of doing well in business is to sell tangible and intangible items and services to people to help them make the most of what they have.

People want to know what the most important lesson that remarkable and successful people learned from life. If you don't want to write to 2,000 billionaires or celebrities, try asking the questions to dedicated teachers and others who spend their lives committed in service. Notice how many more books about the habits of the rich or famous sell than books about poverty. Why do you think people spend money to learn what lessons the rich and famous learned from life? Could it be to view what pitfalls to avoid?

Comments from remarkable people as well as those who are rich and famous are in demand. What sells rapidly are answers to the question of what you've learned from life after achieving stardom, fame, fortune, contentment, serenity, peace, or any other type of success. You could compile all the lessons a lot of famous people learned from life on a videotape and sell it to the self-enhancement video distributors or distribute the tape yourself as a special interest self-enhancement tape.

Making the most of what you have is the surefire way to move ahead one step at a time. While you're moving, you want to look back at your roots to see how you're connected to everyone else. Sure, people want to improve, but they also want to find their roots. And sometimes the paperwork is missing. That's where DNA-driven genealogy kicks in.

A field adjunct to genealogy is DNA-driven genealogy. Although a person can have a background in genealogy, working with a DNA laboratory report stretches the knowledge of the genealogist to learn new fields by reading in the field of molecular anthropology. Historians also would be interested in molecular genealogy.

At each generation, the number of ancestors doubles. Every person has two parents, four grandparents, eight great-grandparents, and sixteen great, great parents. According to the Sorenson DNA Database Web site at: http://smgf.org:8081/pubgen/site19.jsp, "At some point in the past, our ancestors coalesce, and we all share common ancestors. Therefore the total number of actual ancestors for any one person, or group of people is much smaller than the number of possible ancestors. This means that all people in the world are related in varying degrees."

You don't need a degree to prepare attractive covers and brochures which explain in plain language what reports on DNA for ancestry reveal to clients who have their mtDNA or Y chromosomes tested for ancient ancestry. What you need is a bridge to draw from the DNA report and from where the genealogy records stop.

That bridge or time capsule would include a DNA report along with genealogy reports, photos, images, life stories on video disks and tapes, audio recordings, imagery, audio, and text.

Put together in a mega-scrap book, this gift package becomes a time capsule. A time capsule is a new slant on a gift basket to be used by each generation who adds more material and moves the gift basket or container to the next generation. These practical examples are to show you how to make money at home when you need it, working mostly online or through online sales. The objective is to solve a problem for someone, to give benefits, and to show step-by-step procedures on how to achieve results. That's the way to live on less and make money when you need to without a steady job, particularly after your retirement or after age 70+.

Living on less is for everyone at any age. Particularly, it's for those who have retired without a pension, insurance, or much savings and are ages 65-85+. It's also for the younger person starting out and for the growing family that wants to work at home.

Living on less also is for the empty nester who wants to travel for free or stay at home and earn money through play activity. This book is for all those who have no form of employment or income, who are not employed or earning income at the present, and for those who have had to retire without pension, savings, insurance, or security perks. It's for those who simply want to know how they can live on less.

For those with young children, using basic foods costs less. Home schooling may be a family project or a neighborhood project, if a group of families with young children who have similar interests such as science, math, writing, languages, ethnic culture and language, religion, music, or art training join together to home school children with similar interests in that subject—such as music, art/design, journalism, engineering, or science.

I choose (after age 65+) to live on less for the power in the freedom of independent learning and to understand nature. My choice is built around my life-long interest in writing full time and working as an independent contractor in my own home-based online information business.

What does living on less mean to you? Do you want to share communication for income? Living on less for me means never having to retire because you earn money when you want by sharing practical applications of your imagination. Joy and income are derived from sharing information.

Never work when you can play and earn income. In the past, I worked as an educator, spending my days and evenings grading students' communications, English, and writing assignments to earn the same amount that I can earn freelance writing magazine articles, columns, books, and creating courses online or producing life story videos on DVDs.

This type of independence is not for everyone. The choice has to be made: a steady paycheck as a university instructor or little income and no security as a freelance writer? Both choices allow you to remain an educator after retirement.

Would you choose a steady paycheck or the open road as a freelance independent contractor? Do you find joy in balance or extremes?

Sell practical applications of universal archetypes and proverbs. To make money in the media, find out what people fear or love most. Do the opposites paired include the skeleton within versus ageless vigor? Some writers in Hollywood are judged by their youth.

It's different in the world of print media and personal history video. Writers, publishers, and producers in the world of magazines, books, personal history digital video, and newspapers are judged by the wisdom and credibility of their practical information.

The world of text and educational publishing and personal history video welcomes the aged and the hidden. Check out the world of informational how-to publishing.

There are quick ways to make money in order to live on less. Seven of the best ways I found were with my telephone, camcorder, computer, laser printer, software, DVD recorder (re-write) and fast Internet access hookup (DSL). Begin recording significant events or highlights in the stories of peoples' lives.

Everyone enjoys reading or viewing nourishing and significant events or turning points in people's lives. From vocational biographies and corporate success stories to personal and oral history recordings or transcriptions, memoirs and life stories make money in a hurry without the worry of who will hire you.

Visit senior citizens' assisted living apartment complexes lounges and social gathering rooms. Volunteer to record the life stories on tape, CDs, DVDs, and save on digital video disks that can be played in most DVD players, CD players, and/or computers. Save your recordings or transcriptions in various forms such as on tape and disk. Have the transcription in text and photos or slides along with the digital disk. There will be a time when the DVDs no longer play on the advanced equipment in the future.

There's money in transcribing oral history tapes. All these ways to earn money to live on less at home involve dealing with information and research, interviewing people, and recording what makes them want to share meaning. Communication is a gold mine for creating material to sell when you have little or no capital to invest in a business.

You can even have a telephone set up to record people calling in and revealing their life story on the recording tape or digital audio hookup to your computer. The phone calls with the life story experiences could be saved in your computer, recorded or 'burned' to a DVD or CD and saved, copied, duplicated, and sent by mail back to the caller. This is a more *nourishing* take on recording "true confessions or true romances."

What would you charge? A fair fee would be anything from $10 for an hour's talking on a CD or DVD and up. What's the current rate in your area for personal history recordings? You need to check out the professional associations and find out what their members charge as a widely accepted rate in your area to record oral history or to transcribe oral history recordings as backup text. It's important for people to be able to read what they can hear.

What would people be willing to pay? Should you depend on volume and keep the price low? A $10 fee for an hour's voice recording on a CD, plus any shipping charges is fair if you have a large volume business. If you only have a few clients, should you charge $20? Market research determines what people are willing to pay. Your competition with many recording facilities placed in strategic areas may be charging half of what you're asking.

Do market research starting with the personal and oral history professional associations and libraries that handle oral history recordings and transcriptions from tape, CD, or DVD to text. These libraries usually are at various universities. One example is the Bancroft Library at University of California, Berkeley. See their Web site at: http://bancroft.berkeley.edu/. The Bancroft Library's Regional Oral History Office is at: http://bancroft.berkeley.edu/ROHO/.

The Regional Oral History Office is a research program of the University of California, Berkeley, working within The Bancroft Library. ROHO conducts, teaches, analyzes, and archives oral and video history documents in a broad variety of subject areas critical to the history of California and the United States.

ROHO provides a forum for students and scholars working with oral sources to deepen the quality of their research and to engage with the theory, methodology, and meaning of individual testimony and social memory.

The Oral History Association's Web site is at: http://omega.dickinson.edu/organizations/oha/pub_eg.html.

Also check out the International Oral History Association's Web site at: http://www.ioha.fgv.br/. You can research the Association of Personal Historians' Web site at: http://www.personalhistorians.org/.

Ask people who work with clients in recording life stories for oral or personal history what their clients would be willing to pay that seems fair for the average person. Start with senior centers, children's rites of passage ceremonies, graduations, grand openings of stores, baby stores, or wedding planners. If most are only willing to pay $10 or $20, then that's your current rate.

Visit social and senior centers, adult education schools, and classes in genealogy and ask what people think a fair price is for a CD or DVD containing up to an hour of voice recording pertaining to life stories, memoirs, or any other letters, significant events or greetings. The price changes if photos, music, and video are added to the DVD.

If families will pay $10 or $100 to record video on a DVD, then the current rate is what people are willing to pay and still feel comfortable enough to continue buying. Ask for feedback from customers. Ask what the customer thinks a fair price is, and you'll not be overpricing your product.

Start low and ask people what they would pay to record the significant events in a life story of each family member at a different stage of life or during a celebration such as a wedding, bar mitzvah, confirmation, anniversary, graduation, first job, retirement, childbirth video, child's first words or steps recording, or golden years memoirs. You can offer the same services for pet owners with their pets.

You record the highlights of the person's life or how they lived through an event or war, job or economic downturn, upturn, or any significant experience. You can put the video of scenes in the life of a pet, childbirth, children's' first steps and words, or anything else allowable, legal, and ethical on a DVD. It becomes part of a multimedia scrap book or time capsule.

That's how to earn money quick. So the basics on living on less would be your seven-item income-generators in times of emergency—Telephone with voice recording device, fast Internet access hookup such as DSL, computer, laser printer, camcorder, DVD re-write drive recorder (burner) and software.

Create letters, sales flyers, videos on DVDs or CDs, brief audio or video email, brochures, business cards, news releases, and plan budgets for yourself and for clients. Document highlights of life stories as skits, videos, audios, photos, and text transcriptions on DVDs as time capsules or prayer boxes. Or write corporate histories, case histories, and success stories.

Do all this and you can share what you know about how to live on less and make money showing others how to live on less or how to record their personal histories. You don't need a special degree, credential or profession to talk about how to share life's little events. You're marketing practical applications of communication as the sharing of meaning. What about software?

2

Free Software

To get free software, start reviewing software for publications. If you have reviews on your Web site send those to some of those free throwaway computer publications. Show software companies the news clips of your publications and ask for free software review copies. Create stationary and a service whereby you review software and books. You'll get free software and books to review and keep. Always send a tear sheet of the published review to the corporation who sent you the free product to review.

With the review copies of the software, you can print business cards. Keep a review Web site and ask for review copies of books, audio books, software, or anything else to review. You get to keep the product. The manufacturer gets a published review on your Web site and in a few publications to which you send the reviews.

You can eventually even sell the books on eBay as used books after you review them and generate more money. Keep it legal and obey the rules of the software or book publisher.

Form a chain of services and products you can do for others and sell later with their permission. That way you can hold your head high and be proud of helping others, obeying their rules, and generating income for yourself while you live on less. As an example, during the height of the dot.com boom, I wrote corporate success stories and was appointed as freelance case history manager by a software manufacturing company.

I received free software and was paid $500 for every one and a half page article I wrote based on telephone interviews with clients and customers of the software manufacturer who had successfully switched from another brand to the corporation's brand of software. My interview questions were based on the results, problems solved, and step-by-step directions on how they tweaked their computers so that production increased.

The objective focused on writing about what successes resulted from switching to the new software. The brief articles or news releases emphasized results obtained from the new software. I asked the usual questions: "Why did you switch, when, where, how, who, and what?" Answers could be emailed to me after I sent those questions, or could be answered by phone, and with permission, recorded.

Then I typed, edited, and saved on disk the recorded responses. To get approval, I emailed the edited responses, now one-and-one-half page in length. Once the corporation's public relations director gave a go-ahead, I sent the article back to the software manufacturer's public relations and marketing communications directors. This freelance work provided a pretty good income for someone working part-time online at home.

Work had to be play. Benefits included the joy of writing, talking about intellectually stimulating subjects, income based on each page of submitted finished work, and a steady stream of people to interview from a wide variety of occupations.

I created this 'business' by emailing software manufacturers to let them know I'm available to write corporate success stories and case histories they could collect and hand out to selected media who would then take the articles and turn them into business or feature stories for major media publications.

In return the software manufacturer mailed me business cards with my name above the title, "case history manager." The interviewing, writing, and editing experience showed me how to pare down words to bare bones for one-and-a-half page news media releases. Later, I could offer media release writing services for the current freelance fee.

In this way I built up a list of contacts that had approved what I wrote. There are benefits to being a freelance public relations writer of corporate success stories based on case histories. You eventually connect with the credible media and professional journalists' associations. Rapport is by phone and email.

By moving along this route of connections and online conferencing, I created a plan, budget, and map of how to live on less as well as how to generate income in a hurry. Start with the following basic seven pieces of equipment, including a telephone pickup device for recording two-way voice phone conversations (always with permission).

You'll need a voice recording device plugged into the jack on your telephone. Use the fastest Internet access hookup you can afford, such as DSL. You'll need a computer, laser printer, camcorder, DVD re-write drive, and software. Companies gave me everything else such as software, books, or audio books to review. I publicized these companies' products by writing articles for the media. I also wrote news releases for the manufacturer's own corporate communications departments or publications. The same equipment allowed me to write more than 50 published books.

If you want to live on less, enjoy these tips to save or make money. Play in comfort at what works well for you. My requirement for income-generating work is that it should be joy-filled play, especially after age 65. You can enjoy life living on less at any age if you take everything step-by-step and keep applications practical.

Tangible, long-term benefits sell. Always plan for surprises, explore them, and work around and with them. And develop your creativity towards a goal of inspiring others. Budget time before you budget money. List everything that you really like to do. What energizes you the most for the long term? What drains you? Here's how to start.

3

Budgeting Money

If you want to travel at little or no cost to you, travel as an advisor to a company that concerns itself with your specialty. For example, if you're a hairstylist, be an international hairstylist and travel as an adviser for various international hair care and cosmetic companies. Become an expert on emerging trends in your special field—whether it's local and international hair care or cosmetics or DNA testing for ancestry, personal history, or anything else you enjoy doing.

Drop into a variety of cultures and learn what they use for your special field. Create an environment and bring back the information that other firms can use.

The key words are to bring back parts of each culture with you and market the information to manufacturers in your niche.

If you don't like traveling as an adviser, then work online at home bringing new information to companies and trade journals before the media gets that information. You would be looking for new trends.

What's your driving force? Write it in your notebook. Some people's driving force is art and culture. Pick a specific industry—such as DNA testing, music or fashion. Can you sell the work of musicians to the movie industry? Look for new niches where you can tap into many cultures and bring back new information from online interviews or actual travel.

From whom does each company take its cues? What are the forthcoming or current trends in your niche area of expertise or interest? Tap the unexpected trends and sell them in each specialty niche. What's the new look in a hidden place or market? What's the attitude?

Go all over the world by actual travel or virtual reality and online teleconferencing to learn from and teach at various places where your special expertise is taught or used. Ask corporations to let you attend high-profile events where information about new trends is welcome.

Launch a line of products for others. Give others visibility to earn a living. It won't cost you anything to make sure others with money have the visibility they want when the new trend arrives. Coordinate events and activities.

Travel and take notes on applications of new ideas. Decide what type of clients you're trying to find. Raise the standard in your own chosen industry. That's how you can earn a living from living with fewer expenses. Tap into healthier markets. Work with people who purchase for corporations—the buyers.

Help create practical strategies or images for Web sites or press (media) kits where people can buy what you have online. Write down what your vision is, what you'd like to see happen. Put yourself on the cutting edge of your own enterprise.

Have a playful time at living on less for a living. Look at mood, texture, and items that are easy to work with that promote a good attitude. Invest in what is fun for most people and include yourself.

Before you begin to live on less, or plan how to earn income, you need to develop two types of budgets—a money budget and a time budget. How much income each month do you earn?

List what you earn. List what you'll spend. What items are necessary and important? Between the ages of 18 and 48, you're either in school or working and parenting, or all of the above. On a budget of $1,000 a month net (after taxes), from your full-time job, how would you divide your time and money in order to enjoy more while living on less?

Create a Loose-leaf Note Book—A Journal of Priorities.

Your first step is to list your priorities. What's most important to you? Start a loose-leaf notebook for budgeting and journaling. Add pages and dividers for your items. Use a computer, and save your journal files, and budgets. Print out large, readable text with plenty of white space. Keep adding to the three-hole loose-leaf. Use color-coded tabs for each item to organize the notebook.

You need a framework, a foundation, or a basic starting point to organize how much money and time will be divided among your priorities. That notebook will help you deal with the logistics of grouping similar information together in order to get organized.

Not everyone goes to college full time. For those who work and go to school part-time, develop one budget of money and one budget of time.

Put aside enough pages that you can add to create a money budget, and do the same for a time budget.

Here's how to organize such budgets for single persons ages 18-28 in the early stages of climbing the career ladder. Perhaps you attend school part time. Let's assume you work indoors in an office, institution, or retail store. You could be starting out in any type of *entry-level job* earning $8-$12 per hour.

Your first step to living on less would be to budget your time before you budget your income. Your second step is getting creative to generate more income. You can make extra money by healing children with puppets. Use puppets and video to get people to express feelings, imagination, and practical applications of creativity.

4

Budgeting Time

There are only 16 hours of waking time, between 6:00 AM and 10:00 PM. How are you going to divide those 16 hours? Write down your plan or list in the Budgeting Time section of your loose-leaf notebook.

When you see it in writing, it helps you organize your waking hours more effectively than when you don't see a written plan. Be sure to plan enough time to engage in relaxation, exercise, and food preparation for maximum nutrition. How long does it take you to cook nutritious meals? Can you prepare foods ahead and freeze them?

Choose a proverb from a book of proverbs that appeals to you and helps you reach your goals. Work that proverb into your time and money budgets so you can live that proverb daily. Work play therapy into your time budget.

Work with proverbs, quotations, and allegories. Study the techniques of puppeteers. Get out from being bent under the burdens of working full-time, going to school full-time, and rearing families. Do one task at a time. Make a choice of how you are going to spend the years when you are ages 18-28 without having to spread yourself thin. Work and use street smarts, go to school on loans, go to school one course at a time, or save education for middle-age or later if the career you want doesn't require specific training and licenses. For example, if you work full-time and take general liberal arts courses, those courses can be taken later, unless your goal is to teach in college.

Another choice is to postpone having children during the years 18-28 when you attend school full-time and possibly work part-time. You can't work full-time, rear several toddlers as a single parent, and attend college full-time without shortchanging everyone and yourself. Take one step at a time.

Learn time management from puppeteers. Watch how puppets reach out to unlock feelings. Collect puppets or make and sell them. Write skits for puppets. Create puppets that fit on hospital trays. Make puppet stages out of umbrellas with round drapes hanging from them to hide the puppeteer. Make puppet stages that attach to wheelchairs. Create styles of healing while you're young.

Use the techniques of puppeteers and expanded proverbs to plan your time budget, particularly on prioritizing the years from 18-48 with the most important goals finished first. You need a plan and an activity in order to develop hope. Time budgets give you hope.

Your goal is to create a practical application of hope—an activity or behavior that is tangible for the various chunks of time in which you divide waking hours. If your activity or application is practical, then you can launch it. Buyers look for more affordable useful items. How do you budget time to be a useful, practical, tangible object that attracts buyers? Teach people how to grow from doer to leader. Or renovate a house, room, object, or data, figuratively from doer to leader.

Leaders budget their time before they budget their money. Show others how to better budget their time. Point out how budgeting time makes it easier to budget money.

Where do you learn how to budget your own time? First check on what you have accomplished. Then change the structure of your day to accomplish less or more. The structural plans depend upon your health, comfort, and stress level.

Read articles on budgeting time and money. Become knowledgeable about the subject of dividing time into chunks of activity, play, and rest. Study time management and personal budgets. Then share what you've learned.

You can begin by searching the Internet's Web with the key word "time management" at a search engine such as Google at http://www.google.com. You'll see various Web sites or recommended books and articles. Your ultimate goal at any age is to have your assets outweigh your liabilities.

5

Children

Parenting duties consist of reacting to emergencies, troubleshooting emotions, and scrap booking memories. Simultaneously, everyone needs to pull his own weight to support the family financially. How will you keep your family together at a stage of life when you need to go forth in the world? When and how will you become independent? What's your plan for working at eventual interdependence?

The bottom line is that to live on less, you have to find locations to live that cost less—housing, food, and clothing first, then transportation, recreation, and education. Currently, you can live on less in Midwestern urban or rural settings, but can you earn income there or find work? That's when you turn to extreme telecommuting. You can work online at home from any place, but not all jobs have online work at home available.

Turn to the cost of living indexes for various areas of the country and what type of work is available in your field. Before you decide whether or not to have children at your stage of life, make a plan listing and comparing the costs of raising children.

Research the Consumer Price Index (CPI) to find the cost of raising children from birth to age 18. Look for monthly cost tables. Research the annual reports issued by the US Department of Agriculture.

Since 1960, it has estimated the cost of raising a child from birth to age 18, with variations for two-parent and one-parent families; low, middle, and high income levels; different regions of the country; and urban versus rural areas.

Years ago, a US Dept. of Agriculture report stated that in 1997 "Families living in the urban Midwest and rural areas have the lowest child-rearing expenses." If you want to live on less, live in the urban Midwest when you're young. When you're older, you might not be able to tolerate the winters outside Palm latitudes. Will you be able to afford to move to the type of home you need at a location with milder climate? Are you planning for these types of surprises? Research how many retired American couples move to Mexico to live on a budget of $500 a month. Can you interview some of them? Guadalajara is but one area sometimes selected.

Visit your library and read magazines such as *Parents* and *American Demographics.* USDA does not include information on how to live on less. They don't include the cost of insurance for prenatal care, the cost of childbirth or adoption. Have you budgeted for lost income from a parent who stays at home or works less than full time? How are you going to pay for your child's college education?

Think these facts through and list them in your loose-leaf notebook. Would children be better off if they came in your early thirties rather than in your early twenties? Prepare for surprises. Worried about food costs? Look at the Web site of the Center for Nutrition Policy at Promotion at http://www.usda.gov/cnpp/dietary_guidelines.html.

Information on what it costs to raise a child is valuable and can be shared. Serve children during the 18-28 decade. List ways you can make money helping children reach their potential. Don't even think of having children before you prepare a budget listing expenses and time. *Compare* what it costs to rear children against income lost during the decade from ages 18-28.

Consider the cost to you for staying home with children or paying someone to watch your children while you look for a steady job. Ponder the expenses, and plan the alternatives. Your final decision should always reflect your free choice as to what is the healthiest decision for the long term.

Help other people's children heal or express their creativity, imagination, and feelings in useful ways through the arts, music, play therapy, literacy, or science.

The best financial advice for young people is plan on how to live on less and save more during the years up until age 28. Wait until you're in your late twenties to early thirties to start your family. Your late teens to late twenties are your most precious years for receiving an education or starting to move up the ladder in a full-time career or business.

For a woman, having children at ages 28-33 isn't as old as you think. It gives you a decade between age 18-28 to finish your education or save money by working at what comes naturally. Marrying after age 28 helps to keep you out of poverty and makes life less stressful.

You can learn more between ages 18-48 about how to earn and save income or live on less than if you married at 18 and started a family by 21. Think of the expense of rearing three children when you start having children when you're between the ages of 19 and 27. Compare that figure to having a family after working and saving for a decade and then having your family between ages 28-38.

Using your budget, compare what you would have spent for having children between ages 18-27 compared to having worked full-time between ages 18-38 while attending college part time?

Look at the costs of raising children from birth to age 18. What will it cost to support children until the age of 18 in the present decade? Keep the figure posted in front of you. What if you saved that amount with interested for 18 years instead, and then proceeded to have or adopt your family? An increasing number of income-earning women have their first child in their middle to late 30's.

It's true that it's not the most fertile or healthiest time to start bearing, but if the same money is put away for 18 years before starting a family, think of the ability to live on less and in comfort and make a living from living on less and enjoying it by marketing strategies to live on less. The decision is individual. What's more important to you now, and what do you think will be important to you at the start of each decade of your life?

Government information reports and news releases are excellent sources to begin research. For example, a news release emphasizing information in a USDA report is posted at the Web site at: http://www.usda.gov/news/releases/2000/04/0138 titled, "USDA Report Estimates Child Born In 1999 Will Cost $160,140 To Raise." It's listed as Release No. 0138.00.

To find these types of reports, research the USDA's Center for Nutrition Policy and Promotion. According to the USDA report issued in the year 2000, *family income affects child rearing costs, with low-income families projected to spend $117,390; middle-income families $160,140; and upper-income families $233,850 over a seventeen year period. In 1960, a middle-income family could expect to spend $25,230 to raise a child through age seventeen.*

"Housing costs are the single largest expenditure on a child, averaging $53,310 or 33 percent of the total costs over seventeen years. Food was the second largest expense, averaging $27,990 or 18 percent of the total."

Compare these expenses of years ago to what they are today. Then compare these costs against what you would have earned working full-time at an average wage during the decade from ages 19-28. Make a list of pros and cons before you make choices or decisions. Weigh your personal likes and dislikes against the logic of your list of pros and cons. Then make your plan for how to live on less and still enjoy enough comfort and satisfaction to keep you healthy and energized.

How much do you think you could have saved (and put away in an account) in a decade? Figure the amount after all expenses. Make a budget whereby you save from a quarter to a third of your income. Assume you didn't have children until your late twenties. Budget as if you safely invested the money to be spent on expenses you'll have at ages 28-35.

Unless you intend to study full time and go on to graduate school for your career in science, law, and medicine, or related professional work, don't try to combine family life with school and work while you're in that age 18-36 twenty year space of time. Those years are meant for building a fence against poverty for the years 37-57 and beyond and for building your health and stamina.

Don't have children before you have finished all your education. There's enough time from your late twenties to late thirties to start your family without the stress of poverty.

The years from 18-28 should be spent moving up the career ladder, saving, and obtaining experience. The decade before age 26 is the time to devise a plan for living at the comfort level you want to live at during your most productive years.

When you look at government reports, consider that your geographic location determines variations in the cost of raising a child.

Should you live in the Midwest where housing and expenses are less costly than the West? Expenses are highest for families living in the urban West, followed by the urban Northeast and urban South. It's cheapest to live in the urban Midwest. Rural areas have the lowest child-rearing expenses. The source of this information also is found at the Web site containing a USDA press release at: http://www.usda.gov/news/releases/2000/04/0138.

While you're living on less you could research and prepare annual estimates on the cost of raising a child. The USDA does this to help state agencies and courts determine child support guidelines and foster care payments.

Can you find a way to make money doing what the government does and selling your reports to marketing companies? Your reports would have to be more up to date than the government's. Before you think about his, read "Expenditures on Children by Families," at the USDA's Center for Nutrition Policy at Promotion at the Web site: http://www.usda.gov/cnpp.

You need a plan for every stage in life. The idea is to use the plan to work around surprises with enough cushions to support your back so you don't have to watch it.

6

Cleaning Products—Make Your Own Basics

Buy four basic products and make your own cleaning mixes: Instead of detergent, stock washing soda, baking soda, vinegar, and black tea to use for cleaning of different surfaces. Be sure not to use caustic washing soda on aluminum, waxed floors, or fiberglass. Washing soda strips wax.

Make a basic washing mix from a gallon of water and ½ cup of washing soda. For ceramic tile floors, use a gallon of water and a ¼ cup of vinegar. Black tea and water put a shine on your hardwood floors.

Make your own cleaning compounds. You can control the amount of any ingredients you include. Also, you know what you put into the cleaning solutions or mixes that you make from scratch. According to Stony Mountain Botanicals, adding black tea to your floor washing water helps to make floors shiny.

See the Stony Mountain Botanicals Web site: http://www.wildroots.com/natural_cleansers.html.

Black tea mixed with water—about three teabags to a gallon of hot water works well on my hardwood floor. Three tea bags to a gallon of warm water shine a hardwood floor. It's what I experimented with after trying different strengths of tea on my hardwood floor. Don't put tea stains on a light-colored hardwood floor. Wash your tea-colored hardwood floors with black tea.

My hardwood floor is close to the color of a regular cup of black tea. Don't use a lot of water on hardwood. Water turns hardwood floors black. The water is absorbed and bows the wood or rots it. Water makes the wood swell.

Instead, clean off the dirt with a little water and black tea. Then use an oil-based hardwood floor cleaner to protect the wood.

Black tea in water works best on hardwood floors when very little water is used on the wood. For ceramic tile in the kitchen or bathroom, use a micro-mop first to remove all dust and scratchy debris before you wash with vinegar and water. Wash ceramic tile floors with a half cup of vinegar mixed with each gallon of water.

Click on the Do It Yourself Network at http://www.diynet.com/diy/lv_household_tips/article/0,2041,DIY_14119_2275102,00.html. Check out the cleaning tips from Linda Cobb. For example, you can clean ceramic tile floors with water, but don't use a sponge because it drags the grime into the grout. Use a micro mop or vacuum the dirt first before you wash the floor. Check out the Do It Yourself Network Fact Sheet PDF files at: http://www.ncta.com/guidebook_pdfs/DIY.pdf.

Make your own ceramic tile floor washing mixes by mixing a quarter cup of ammonia with a quarter cup of Borax mixed in a gallon of water. Or wash the floor with plain water. Check out Linda Cobb's Queen of Clean Web site for tips on how to clean and make your own cleaning mixes at: http://www.queenofclean.com/tips/index.html and http://www.queenofclean.com/. You can make so many of your own cleaning mixes easily from simple ideas such as a little white vinegar in water in your washing machine or use plain water for simple ceramic tile floor washes. She has excellent cleaning tips such as using unseasoned meat tenderizer as a stain remover or tips on conquering clutter. I highly recommend these tips. They have saved me so much money by creating my own cleaning products from simpler and less costly, less processed materials.

If Linda Cobb, the *Queen of Clean*, can create a TV show and books on how to clean and organize, you too can find ways to share and experience living the more unprocessed and balanced life.

Why Washing Soda?

The generic term, "washing soda" with a pH of 11, is a salt. Washing soda is sodium carbonate and a lot more caustic than baking soda, although it is a soda processed to be a lot more alkaline and caustic enough for you to wear protective gloves to protect your hands. There are no harmful fumes. To buy washing soda, check the laundry shelves in supermarkets. Use a generic brand from your supermarket or a brand such as Arm & Hammer.

Baking soda is less caustic. It's called sodium bicarbonate. You also can make generic or basic cleaning mixes and compounds using baking soda. Besides putting an open box of baking soda in your refrigerator to get rid of odors, you can use it as a cleaner. Wear your gloves when you handle anything with baking soda and washing soda. Alkaline products are caustic to the skin. Never use washing soda the way you use baking soda.

You'll use washing soda to get rid of soot after a fire or to cut grease and oil. Washing soda will strip wax or lipstick and other oily coatings. It's good for getting rid of petroleum oil. It's not for fiberglass. To make a generic cleaner, mix a bucket of warm water with ½ of washing soda. For a less caustic cleaner, mix a bucket of warm water with ½ cup baking soda. Baking soda is a bit less caustic on the hands, but gloves are recommended because of the sodium and the alkaline effect on your skin.

Whenever you wash with baking soda or washing soda, always rinse whatever you washed, and keep wearing your gloves. If you want a generic drain cleaner, put white vinegar down the drain followed by baking soda. Let the fizz come up and then rinse well after the fizzing stops.

You can make a paste of baking soda or washing soda and water. Spread paste on soot or other dirt and put a mixture of either baking or washing soda in a spray bottle with water, mix, and spray. Leave on for a few hours and rinse thoroughly. Only use this mixture on glass or stone. Remember that washing soda usually peels off paint as well as wax.

Home-Made Deodorant

If you want to make your own deodorant without artificial additives such as aluminum, just take a teaspoon of baking soda, a pinch of cornstarch, and a dab of petroleum jelly. Mix the petroleum jelly with the baking soda and a pinch of cornstarch.

When it looks like a facial cream or smoothes on like a cream, use it under your arms. It works better if you swab the area with rubbing alcohol first and then apply the petroleum jelly and baking soda mix with a little cornstarch to make it go on smoother. Wash this off after a few hours. Don't use petroleum jelly near your nostrils.

Make your own hard soap from recipes on the Internet's World Wide Web starting at Miller's Homemade Soap Pages at: http://www.millersoap.com/ and also at: http://www.millersoap.com/soapproc.html.

Also check out the home made soap recipe at this other Web site at: http://nvnv.essortment.com/homemadesoaps_rbzq.htm. When you make soap, you might make an olive oil and grape seed oil soap.

How Do You Make A Basic Face And Bath Soap?

It's amazing what you can make with glycerin. Use it to get out stains from clothing by soaking glycerin and water on the spot. Or add a teaspoon of glycerin to soaps and home-made shampoos to add a moisturizing, lotion-like effect. Can you make soap for yourself at less cost than buying it commercially at the market? Yes, if you have the time to make soap, including melting the bits of soap you already have and remolding it or making soap from scratch. You have control over the scent and ingredients. If you want a soap to smell like your favorite scent, make your own soap and add your favorite scent and oils, such as roses and olive oil.

Why make home-made soap with lard when you can make soap with herbs, vegetable oils, or beeswax? Make soap containing almond meal, oat meal, or other ingredients. You can even sell your soap or put in gift baskets.

Soap can be made cheaply in the old fashioned way or creatively with olive and grape seed oils. It's all about what you want to do with your soap, use it frugally yourself. Sell special hand-made soaps as gifts to earn money at home. When you make soap from scratch, using a cold process, you're performing *saponification*. This is a chemical process which converts most types of fat into soap by reaction with an alkali called lye.

Use distilled water when making soap. Soap-making kits are for sale online. All of these kits and special soaps with expensive ingredients are fine. Check out the soap making supplies at: http://www.soapmakersupplies.com/soapmaking/Index.html. You can spend more money buying soap making supplies, kits, and making expensive soaps to sell or use for yourself. Or you can live on less by making soap cheaper than you'd pay for commercial soap. What you have is control over the ingredients.

Compare what it cost you to make soap to what you spend to buy commercial soap. Depending upon the ingredients you put into the soap, home-made soap can be made for less, if you have the time and want to work with the ingredients such as lye and certain fats, beeswax, or olive oil. See the Web site at: http://www.soapmakersupplies.com/soapmaking/HowTo_ColdProcess.html for making basic cold-process soap using either fats or oils.

The SoapMakersSupplies.com Web site at: http://www.soapmakersupplies.com/soapmaking/HowTo_ColdProcess.html lists these **Soap Making Supplies Needed:**

Oils (fats)
Caustic Soda (lye)
Distilled Water
Newspaper
Safety Glasses or Goggles
Rubber or Plastic Gloves
Scale
Glass Jar
1 Lye Pitcher (plastic). Mark pitcher and use it only for lye water
Long-handled Wooden Spoon
2 Thermometers (one for oils and one for lye water)
Stainless Steel Soap Pot (do not use aluminum pot)

Mold. Use a Plastic or Wood Box or other Container
Insulating Materials (blankets work well)
Freezer or Butcher Paper
Fragrance or Essential Oils
Colorant

When at Soap Maker Supplies Web site, click on one of the site's soap-making recipes. You can choose the cold process or the melting process. If you want to make soap from scratch the way it was done in the past, choose the cold process method.

The melting process involves simply melting soap you already have and re-shaping it or adding scents, textures such as oatmeal or almond meal, and oils—for example olive or grape seed oil. You can melt soap by putting it in a sealed plastic bag and heating it in 120 degree F. water. The cold process of making soap from scratch requires that you work with lye and fats or oils.

Lay out all the ingredients and equipment first before starting. Don't forget essentials such as safety glasses, vinyl or latex gloves, and a water and vinegar solution for washing and neutralizing any caustic lye that touches you or other equipment.

Other Web sites list similar supplies needed. Check out the soap-making recipes at the Pioneer Thinking Web site at: http://www.pioneerthinking.com/soaps.html

You can start from scratch and make your own soap using lye and fats as people did in historic times. Or you can grate a bar of ivory soap with a cheese or potato grater and then melt it in a pan over a very low heat adding food flavorings such as vanilla or almond. Add any scent that appeals to you and pour the melted soap into a bowl. You can add oat meal and chopped nuts or a scent of jasmine, lavender, melon, or musk oil perfume. The scent would be expensive, though. Artificial vanilla would be more frugal. These hand-made soaps can be put in gift baskets. You also can add olive oil or grape seed oil to your soaps.

If you're starting from scratch, you'll need to use lye. You can't make soap without lye unless you make soap out of your old bits of soap such as pan-melted ivory soap with added ingredients such as meal (oat meal) or scents. You also can use an old bottle of rose cologne or rose-petal water, orange-blossom water, or any type of safe and healthy scent that doesn't cost more than the original soap.

Here's how to make lye soap from scratch. Since lye is caustic and has extremely bad fumes, keep the lye away from children and use a child-proof cover on its container. Lye burns skin. Don't touch it with your hands. If you want to make your own soap from scratch, here is the recipe. The Pioneer Thinking Web site at: **http://www.pioneerthinking.com/soaps.html** lists the following soap making supplies needed:

Ingredients:

1 can (12 oz or 340 grams) Lewis Red Devil 100% lye

21 1/2 oz (605 grams) ice cold or part frozen *distilled* water

5 lbs, 7 1/3 oz (2.48 kg) lard or all vegetable shortening. You can add olive oil or grape seed oil. Any type of vegetable shortening works well. Use the type of hard fat that you feel comfortable with knowing the finished soap comes in contact with your skin.

Equipment:

1 each of 1-2 quart Pyrex or oven ware bowl

1 each of a 4-6 quart plastic bowl or stainless or cast iron pot

1 each of plastic, wooden or stainless big spoon

1 each of shallow cardboard box lined with plastic trash bag

Latex or vinyl gloves

Canning pot (for water bath if you use plastic reaction bowl)

Instructions:

Prepare a wooden or plastic box to be used as a mold that won't allow hot liquid fat to leak out. Line it with plastic such as a transparent painter's drop sheet cut to size or a plastic garbage bag or cat litter box liner. I like to use a square of plastic painter's drop cloth that comes on a roll, which I can cut to fit the box. You can cut it to fit the inside of the box and the outside, so there are no seams with openings for liquids to spill out. Check the box by putting water in it first to make sure there are no leaks. Then spill out the water. Put the box aside.

Keep handy a container of water mixed 10% with vinegar and a sponge to neutralize what splashes on you or on any surface. Remember that lye is alkaline and caustic. To neutralize the burning effects of lye, you need vinegar, which is an acid that won't burn you if it splashes on you when mixed with water. (Use 10 percent vinegar and 90 percent water in your solution.)

Keep that vinegar mixture in a container handy whenever you work with lye nearby. When you mix acid with alkaline, the effect is to neutralize the burning, caustic alkaline lye that splashes on you or on your furniture or clothing.

Put on your vinyl or latex gloves and any goggles to protect your eyes from caustic chemical splashes. Freeze half of your water into ice cubes. Put the ice cubes and the rest of the water into the 1 to 2 quart bowl. Use the stirring spoon (known to soap makers as the 'crutch'). Add the lye very slowly to the ice and water, stirring until the lye is all dissolved. Go slowly.

If the lye splatters on you, it will burn you. Immediately wash with a mixture of 10 percent vinegar and 90 percent water to neutralize the caustic alkaline lye. Place next to you that bottle of water mixed with vinegar to neutralize and washing any lye that touches you or any other surface on which you're working.

Lye gives off caustic fumes. Make sure the window is open and the room ventilated. Keep pets and children out of the room. Use a fume-proof cover over the solution. You don't want to expose the solution to air. Let it rest until it reaches 85 degrees F. You can cover the pot with a glass cover. Keep glass, plastic, or wooden covers for the working pot or the box in which the soap hardens. Don't let anything stay exposed to the open air.

Use a glass bowl or pot, never aluminum or galvanized metal. You're working with hard fats such as vegetable shortening. Melt the fat in the 4-6 quart bowl or pot. When the fat is melted, cool it down to 95 degrees F. Don't pour anything into your lined box yet. You're still working with your large glass pot.

Put aside your wooden box to use as a square mold. Line the box with plastic transparent or plastic trash bag lining. Make sure the liquid soap when poured into your wooden box that will be used as a mold, will not spill or leak in any way. You're dealing with hot liquid, melted fat.

You're box is put aside, and now you're still working with the ingredients in your large glass pot. Into the pot, stir the liquid fat in a clockwise direction while pouring the lye water into it in a stream so thin that it looks like a skinny pencil. After all the lye water is added to the liquid fat, stir the mix using an "s" pattern. Soap makers use the verb "to crutch" instead of "to mix." Use a circular pattern. You also can use a hand blender as long as the circular pattern is repeated until the mix cools and slightly thickens. Keep stirring. If you stop, the mix separates.

The mix will begin to take on the consistency of cream and then thicken to look more like a pudding. Keep stirring from 10 to 45 minutes. If you use a hand blender, you'll be able to stop stirring much sooner. To tell when it's time to stop, dribble a stream from your stir stick. The batch should show traces. How long it takes for your soap to thicken depends upon the ingredients and the temperature in your work room or kitchen.

Many home-made soap crafters say that pure ingredients take less time, perhaps 10 minutes. Your trace is what appears when you dribble a stream from your stirring stick onto the liquid in the middle of your pot. What you want to see in your trace is the dribble from the stream that drips from your stirring stick. Make sure the dribble doesn't drown into the surface.

If the dribbled stream doesn't sink, then the soap is ready to pour into the lined box. Careful—wear rubber gloves and treat the raw soap like you treated the lye water. Wash off all splatters immediately. Now you're carefully pouring your soap into your lined box.

Cover your box to keep out the air. Use a wooden or plastic cover. Let stand for three to five hours. Then cut into bars with a dull table knife. Never use a sharp knife. Allow the soap to cure in the box for about a week before breaking it up and handling it, and another month before using it.

Centuries ago, the early New England settlers on farm wives who made soap actually put their tongues on the new bars of hardened soap to see whether the unreacted lye burned. Don't try this because it's unknown how it will affect your ability to taste or your taste buds. The soap that this recipe makes can be used for your face or for bath soap. You can add olive or grape seed oil in small amounts while the fat is liquid.

There's another kind of soap that was used in the past for washing floors called Lye Soap. It uses less fat. One recipe asks for 5 pounds, five ounces of fat, and the soap had to rest for six months before using it. Don't use lye soap on your face. The more fat and oils such as olive oil, grape seed oil, or face creams you put into your soap, the more suitable it becomes for face and bath use.

For colorful soap, you can add food coloring or non toxic children's tempura paint powder—about 20 grams, according to one recipe on the Web at: the Home Made Soap Recipe site at: http://nvnv.essortment.com/ homemadesoaps_rbzq.htm. You add the coloring when the soap mix reaches the heavy cream stage, according to the Web site mentioned above. My feeling is that soap touches your skin and is absorbed somewhat. So I wouldn't want to put nontoxic tempura paint powder into soap that constantly touches my skin.

Instead, my personal feeling is that safe food coloring or coloring from vegetables such as spinach juice, beet juice, or similar natural food colorings used in foods would be preferable. You can try various colorings made from natural vegetables that are labeled safe to eat. This is not because you're eating the soap, but because it contacts your skin and pores.

Not everyone likes scented soap. If you want a scent, such as vanilla or almond, orange or rose, you can add about two ounces (60 grams) of rose petal or orange blossom water, jasmine, vanilla, almond, or other scented essential oil or perfume before the soap is thick enough to pour.

Another way of added scent is to finish curing the soap. According to the Home Made Soap Recipe site, you can dip a muslin cloth in scented oil and wrap it around the soap. Then seal in the scent with aluminum foil.

I like to use rose petal water and rose petal extract scented oil. I dip a cloth in the rose petal scented oil. Then I wrap the cloth tightly in plastic and keep it airtight for two months. The Web site recommends wrapping the soap in muslin dipped in scented oil and then wrapping that in aluminum foil for six weeks. Your objective is to have the perfume sink into the soap all the way to its core and not just on the outer layer.

When I want to change the form of the bar of soap, I put the bar of soap into a plastic bag that seals tightly. Then I lower the soap into hot water (120 degrees) for a half hour. That makes the soap soft enough to cut and roll into balls or press into a mold. My favorite molds are animal figures or oval shapes. When the soap cools, it hardens. After reshaping, let the soap rest for a few hours.

You can melt down most types of soaps, even glycerin soaps that are translucent. Any type of hard soap can be melted and remolded to a new shape. An interesting shape is to make a mold of your portrait in three dimensions, like a sculpture and give soap bars as gifts molded into the shape of someone's face.

7

Clothing

Buy shelf-pulls. Look for surplus clothing from overstocked wholesalers, warehouses, and liquidators. Look for clothing and other items returned to department stores that sell at a deep discount at warehouses. Shop for surplus goods, close outs, and liquidation items. One example of a one-stop shop surplus warehouse is Via Trading Corporation. The company's Web site is at: http://www.viatrading.com/.

If you want to live on less and make a living that way, consider selling on eBay or your own Web site products that are drop-shipped to you. Also check out the flea markets, swap meets, and garage sales. You can buy clothing or books very inexpensively at garage sales. Buy by the pallet and not by the piece.

Keep what you need and sell the rest online at eBay or other Web sites or at swap meets, garage sales, or throw clothing parties with your friends, neighbors, or relatives to sell clothing, especially children's clothing or other items. Buy items in bulk, including clothing, if you will need it. It's cheaper to buy in bulk.

New merchandise that's surplus or overstocked sells in warehouses at a huge discount. The surplus is sold both to the public and to those who resell the products or clothing online or at swap meets. Also check out the clothing or electronics brokers. When you buy an item, ask whether you can pay the reseller's price.

That way you can buy several of the same items at that price, keep an item for yourself and sell the rest online such as on eBay. It pays to get a business license from your local Board of Equalization as a reseller of the items you want to purchase to keep one, and resell the rest.

Is making your own clothing too time consuming? You'd have to spend money for a sewing machine, patterns or pattern supplies, thread, needles, scissors and other sewing equipment. Where else can you get *quality* clothing that lasts as long as you need it— for less? Second-hand stores that handle "upscale neighborhood" clothing are fine if you don't mind cleaning the clothes all over again when you get them home.

No one is suggesting you look for clothing in dumpsters. However, some astute dressers actually look over designer clothing and fabrics from dumpsters in upper class neighborhoods or from the discarded samples of fashion design salons, manufacturers and designing schools. Clothing from upper-East Side NY trash bins may be searched for throwaway wearable clothing and usable items.

There's usually someone hunting for discarded fabrics from wholesalers and remnants from fabric stores. Many second hand or thrift shops depend upon people that bring in clothes. Not all people bring in cleaned clothing, although stores usually ask you to have a garment cleaned before you donate it. Where else can you look to buy new clothes that don't fall apart quickly?

Track down the less costly imports along with those made locally from the discount clubs, wholesalers, and surplus stores that buy clothing as well as food and other items in bulk. Also try eBay at http://www.eBay.com. New as well as used clothing and fabrics are bargains if you watch the shipping and handling costs.

Try some of the military surplus stores for clothing and equipment such as Army-Surplus.com at: http://www.army-surplus.com/. Surplus military clothing such as walking boots, camping gear, jackets, and pants generally take more wear and tear than similar department store bought clothing. Try the Army Surplus Online Super Store at the Web site: http://www.army-surplus.com/ss_store/index.html. Check out the duffle bags, boots, and bags.

8

Contacts

The Simple Living Network
http://www.simpleliving.net/
http://www.simpleliving.net/ecoliving/default.asp

Your Money or Your Life Online Study Networks—A Nine-Step Program
http://www.simpleliving.net/ymoyl/default.asp

Study Groups Database
http://www.simpleliving.net/studygroups/default.asp

Building Sustainable Communities http://www.simpleliving.
net/ecoliving/community-default.asp?title=Building+Sustainable+Communities

Manual for Group Facilitators
http://www.simpleliving.net/ecoliving/community-default.asp?title=Manuals

Simple Living Resources Database
http://www.simpleliving.net/resources/default.asp

EscapeArtist.com (Moving to Thailand)
http://www.escapeartist.com/Thailand/Thailand.html

Mother Earth News. Com
http://www.motherearthnews.com/index.php?page=main&ref=mothermisc

Choosing a Log Home (article)
http://www.motherearthnews.com/article/2151/

Log Homes and Log Cabins from Scratch
http://www.loghomebuilders.org/
Also: http://www.loghomebuilders.org/articles_about_log_homes.htm

9

Contracts

USA Contract Categories
http://www.lawdepot.com/contracts/usa/?pid=google-contracts_usa-contracts_b

Legal Database
http://www.legal-database.com/contractlaw.htm

Find Legal Forms.com—Easy to Use Legal Forms for the Right Job
http://www.findlegalforms.com/xcart/customer/home.
php?partner=google&alphabetical=yes

Consumer Report
http://consumerreport.ca/

ConsumerReports.org
http://www.consumerreports.org/main/home.jsp

ConsumersUnion.org
http://www.consumersunion.org/

10

Creativity

Branding is your mark of creativity. Create a title for yourself and your experience of living on less to make a living. For example, Linda Cobb is known professionally as The Queen of Clean. She writes excellent, helpful books on how to organize, clean, and remove clutter. And she has her own TV show featuring tips on how to clean and make your own cleaning products from less costly materials such as vinegar, borax, ammonia, water, and unseasoned meat tenderizer for removing stains.

Her books and shows feature an enormous number of helpful tips that save money and work right on the materials they clean or organize. For example, there are tips such as when sitting at the dinner table, as soon as something spills on your clothing or carpet, putting salt on stains from gravy or food takes out the stains in an emergency. Club soda removes red wine, coffee, tea, and even red pop soda if you put it on the stain right away.

What all these tips show is practical creativity. You can live on less and make a living at it by sharing creativity about your helpful, practical applications that show people how to improve and simplify their lives through step-by-step useful how-to information.

To express creativity about living on less and sharing the experiences, first create your own logo, title, and plan of how you will share useful information. Will you be the next ogre of organization, curmudgeon of clutter, duke of drains, prince of plumbing, or cloisonné of clean? Will you be the next earl of examples, marques of mothering, sovereign of simplicity, viscount of ventilation, lady of less, sultan of sources, sheik of shopping, or baron of bargains? You get the picture.

Put creativity into the elbow work. Use a term that's familiar to many or a proverb that you expand into **branding.**

11

Comparison Shopping

Pay Less for High-Quality Items and Services Using Focused Practical Comparison Shopping Strategies

High-quality bargains emphasize simplicity and commitment. The more creative you become, the more you need to simplify your life style. Simplicity sells because it offers commitment to basic values. To be more creative in purchasing and saving, simplify your lifestyle. Make the complex clearer to understand.

To sell your concept of living on less, getting what you pay for, simplifying your life, or bargain-hunting in hidden markets, you need to develop buzz appeal. You have to package your strategies, tips, and techniques to the media in a way that has universal appeal. What you're marketing is a concept.

The concept emphasizes simplicity, commitment, and time-tested values. This concept is all about making what is difficult to understand clear and easier to understand. You're looking for a concept that unites everyone, a type of simplicity that is universal, with which nearly everyone can identify.

You're looking for a concept that gives people the power to choose what helps them reach their maximum potential, make their own decisions, and think about what's right. You want a concept that makes people feel good about themselves and important. What's that concept? It's getting what you pay for.

Everyone wants a bargain as long as the bargain is of high quality and long-lasting. You want to live the concept of living on less and having more. More what? You're emphasizing quality of life. Your bargains represent products or ideas that stand up to the test of time. In your concept of you get what you pay for, emphasize better quality when it comes to wear and tear.

12

Branding

How do you live on less, have more, and get what you pay for? You emphasize simplicity and commitment. That's what you market in your buzz appeal campaign to the media and to the public as your customers and clients.

Your first step would be to use branding to make a 'brand' or trade name or logo and slogan for yourself that represents your basic concept and message. That's a proverb or quotation that in one sentence or less tells the public what you represent, to what you are committed. Keep it simple and short. After you have your branding complete with slogans and proverbs, launch your *get what you pay for* theme in the media.

To select a reporter from the media, find out by reading publications and newspapers who is writing a story similar to your concept or who has recently written a similar article. That reporter may not do another similar story, but can refer you to someone who might. Call the features editor and ask who has written similar articles or will be assigned a similar topic on bargain hunting for quality, getting what you pay for, simplifying your life, or living on less, saving, and enjoying the lifestyle more.

If you emphasize extreme telecommuting, travel, working outdoors, mobile lifestyle, working at home, or any other lifestyle, work style or attitude, focus on publications that emphasize publishing information or advertising those types of products.

If your writing is honest and dramatic, it will appeal to the newspaper reporter who is writing on a subject similar to yours. If that reporter from a national newspaper or other national publication with a very wide circulation writes about your story or interviews you and incorporates passages into the reporter's piece, quoting your story—fiction or biography—you have a great chance of publishers and agents contacting you. Usually, it will be an agent who is willing to bid your story to publishers.

Here's a famous example. Jessie Lee Foveaux, at the age of 98, sold her memoir for a million dollars, and she had never published before. She sold her book and movie rights. Was it luck or buzz appeal? The Life of Jessie Lee Brown from Birth up to 80 years had been written in longhand for an adult education class in writing for senior citizens writing their life stories.

In fact, she wrote the book manuscript 18 years before it found a market. How did she get it auctioned to competing book publishers and movie producers? How did she find her agent? Her life story is all about how she, as a battered wife married to an alcoholic husband, managed to raise eight children alone after leaving her husband and how hard she struggled to put food on the table. It is because she is from Kansas and spent her time knitting cross-shaped bookmarks for her church members that the story had universal appeal to agents?

The message of the book emphasized commitment and simplicity. It's hard to find an agent who would take on a 98-year old great, great grandma and sell her life story for a million dollars. Foveaux wrote her memoir back in 1979 when friends encouraged her to enroll in an adult education writing class. Her writing teacher, who also is a farmer, gave out assignments to the senior citizens in the class to write the story of their lives.

Foveaux even protested to her writing teacher at adult school that she didn't have the time to write. He insisted that she make the time and encouraged her to write. She took his advice and brought in her assignments each week with up to four thousand words of her life story.

When you try to sell simplicity and commitment in any item, whether it's your diary or a gift basket of hand-made products, write down what's different about what you have to offer? Foveaux wrote the details of how she spent her childhood, the characters who inhabited towns in which she lived, and details of her relatives.

Then she started on a narrative and got to the deeper story of her life. That's what you have to do—get to the deeper story of how to get what you pay for. Details and information are what sells—the facts and how to apply them in a practical, yet simple way to improve. Foveaux wrote about commitment using a simple plot with lots of details of her life story. She worked as a grocery clerk and other jobs to support all her children.

What in this story differed from the thousands of memoirs that are written by seniors in adult education classes? It's this story that brought in a million dollars from publishers, plus movie rights. How did this story differ from the others? The visibility or "buzz" appeal began with Foveaux's writing teacher who put her writing in his newsletter that contained the writing of all the students in the senior citizen writing class.

When we analyze how the first step led to the next, we have to look at her writing teacher's credibility adding to her credibility by publishing the writing of all the students in a newsletter. Normally, that would have been the end of the line. Except, by mailing the newsletter to a reporter from The Wall Street Journal, this reporter wrote about the author. That article published in the Wall Street Journal helped to give visibility and credibility to significant highlights of the book. The book soon sold to major publishers for a lot of money.

So you have to have a similar leap from adult education class newsletter of writing to actually being published in a national publication that has national credibility. The most important step of buzz appeal occurred when the Wall Street Journal reporter actually took a step forward to make Foveaux's writings known to the wider world of Wall Street Journal readers.

Your approach and product or attitude needs to be the perfect forum for a particular newspaper or magazine or other media venture. There had to be a reason why the newsletter went to this particular reporter at The Wall Street Journal. After all, most people think of The Wall Street Journal as a financial newspaper full of articles on stocks, investments and mergers. The newspaper's focus is far removed from a senior citizen's memoirs of raising a large family in an unhappy marriage, yet it made the perfect forum because it has universal appeal.

The writing teacher had read a previous article in The Wall Street Journal by that reporter who wrote an in-depth article on senior citizens that attracted the interest of the writing teacher in the Midwest. He sent the article to the reporter because it emphasized the *commitment to family and faith.* To create buzz, your writing, product, or application of your idea *must have some redemptive value to a universal audience.* That's the most important point.

What you need for your idea is *momentum.* You need to have a practical application—details, facts, and step-by-step instruction people can follow in what you present to the public. The Wall Street Journal reporter drew close to the writings of the 98-year old woman. Those writings had such redemptive value to create buzz (universal appeal). The Wall Street Journal reporter developed more buzz (appeal) around the manuscript by writing an article about the author and the manuscript.

Momentum resulted. The momentum moved it along the pipeline so that all the right connections had access by reading the Wall Street Journal. The point is if you want to reach all the right connections for your applications of ideas, you need a pipeline, a publication or other media that is credible enough for the people in power to view.

Make sure the people you want to reach read or view the publication or media to which you send your promotional writings. Do these people you want to reach even read or watch the media that is publishing your work? Before you launch anything in the media, think about who you want to reach.

Do these powerful people actually see that publication daily? Would they be interested in your information on how to get what you pay for or how to live on less and enjoy it more? Would you be better off sharing information not on how to live on less, but on strategies that the wealthy and famous use to get richer and happier at the same time? Think about it. Two very simple values sell to the rich and poor alike. They emphasize commitment. Those two values are *doing the best you can* under the circumstances, and *trusting in your faith*. It's like the old proverb, "You know that I care more than you care what I know."

A front-page story ran in the Wall Street Journal on March 7, 1997. Offers from publishers immediately flooded the writer. A lawyer hired by the writer's relative helped to find a literary agent to look at all the publisher's offers and select the best one. When 20 publishers called and 20 movie producers, offering six-figure movie contracts, the power of buzz—of **credibility** created through **visibility** in the major national press—spun into action.

The point is that without "buzz" (as they say in the publishing world), would that book have gotten the attention it deserved before the author had an agent? If you sent a book manuscript directly to a publisher, it most likely would come back with a note that unsolicited manuscripts are not read.

You'd most likely be told to find a literary agent willing to send your book to publishers. That manuscript might stay on the agent's desk for a year before you finally received it back with a rejection form letter. Who wants to spend that many years trying to find an agent who thinks your book will earn a commission or sell widely?

No matter how great your idea or product is, unless you find someone to buzz you into the national press, you aren't going to be noticed that easily. That's where creativity plays a role. Forget the cliché of thinking outside the box. Instead view the familiar box from a different angle.

To be more creative, find out what's in vogue. What's the current interest? Simplicity and commitment always is in vogue, but you need the next step—time. Look at trends. Research the trends to find out whether what you have to offer is coming at a time when people are trying to hold a family together and put bread on the table at the same time. Now get even more creative. You have buzz appeal.

What you have offers *simple* solutions. Focus more narrowly. Are you appealing to American women? Do the trends say that this is the time when American women are working to support families? What practical steps can you offer them to make life and work easier, less costly, and of better quality?

Foveaux's book was auctioned at more than a million dollars, and Warner cast the top bid. Think about how the author's manuscript went through certain steps to get to the person at Warner with the power to make things happen for the author. Think of what happened in between, the lawyer who helped the auction to happen and the publishers who took an interest. What made all these people take an interest? Look at the value of your writing or information. Is what you have *simple* enough to sell for a million dollars? It has to be really simple to make so much money. Simple means *understandable*, and that's buzz (universal) appeal.

If you want to make a living by living on less, share what's simple and earthy about what you have and what you do. Be yourself. Publishers can spot phoniness in a minute. Can your customers or clients do the same?

If you write, be a real person in your writing. Be true to yourself. What's worth a million? The book emphasized morals, faith, and values. If you analyze what powerful publishers buy for universal appeal, it's a steady focus on values. Publishers look for faith in something greater than our lives. They seek stories of commitment and simplicity of values.

Publishers who buy a book or any other item on its buzz value are buying simplicity. It is simplicity that sells and nothing else but simplicity. This is true for computers, MP3 players, books, or items that have to be assembled by the buyer. Simplicity sells in instructional manuals and in how-to kits. It's good storytelling to say it simply. People want user-friendly gadgets, stories, and information.

Simplicity means what you have to offer gives your customer all the answers everyone looks for in exotic places, but finds close by. What's the great proverb that sells anything to anyone? It's to stand on your own two feet and put bread on your own table for your family.

Living on less and enjoying it more or you get what you pay for are moral points telling you to pull your own weight. And pulling your own weight is a buzz word that sells any product or application of an idea that teaches and reaches through simplicity.

The backbone of the media emphasizes the values of simplicity, morals and faith (or trust). These are universal values. Doing the best to take care of your family sells. That's the buzz appeal you need to emphasize.

Consumers and publishers go through fads every two years—angel books, managing techniques books, computer home-based business books, novels about ancient historical characters or tribes, science fiction, children's programming. The genres shift emphasis, but values are consistent in the bestselling books, toys, and any other product.

You need to offer simplicity, values, morals, and commitment in whatever you want to share to make a living. Look at trends. To live on less and have more, find the highways to simplicity. Target those values. Emphasize commitment.

Buzz is universal, but you need national press to get publishers bidding. National press gives you credibility in the eyes of major publishers. The world is impressed by front page coverage in The Wall Street Journal because of what it symbolizes—stability, dependability, security, centeredness.

Find a newspaper article that relates to what information you want to share. Write to the reporter covering the feature. Query to see whether there is an interest in your story or feature. Make sure you have a new angle on your project. Does your item emphasize universal values, morals, simplicity, and commitment?

Does it span real history in a way that reads and works well? Quality is the most important trait. Visibility and credibility give your product momentum. Buzz appeal gives momentum to the practical application of your idea. Universal values and simple lifestyles sell each time they solve problems, give results, and offer benefits with balance.

Resources: Simplicity, Balance, & Commitment

Living the Simple Life
http://www.cottagesoft.com/~cynthia/nfbkrevw/simplife.htm

Books and Magazines about Balance
http://www.marciaconner.com/fav/balancereading.html

Right on the Money
http://www.rightonthemoney.org/shows/116_simplify/

13

Decorating & Design

Make a budget of money and of time. Set aside another 20 percent to cover expenses if you go over the budget. Live on less by making your own decorations and designs from scratch. To make a table, use a polished thick tree trunk with a flat bottom and top for a middle base and an oval piece of wood for the top. For drapes use easy-to-clean vertical blinds. Make curtains out of colorful sheets. Or sew scraps together like a patch quilt to make tapestry hangings for the walls.

You can use stencils to paint murals on your walls to give the feeling of a larger room. For example, a seascape or trees with perspective give an in-depth feeling of distance. An open road painted on a wall or mirrors from floor to ceiling give the impression that the room is larger.

Paint your walls white and stencil murals if you want to give the impression of depth perspective. Look at the walls of restaurants painted in murals of balconies and palm trees with a seascape in the distance.

Work on the kitchen and bath. The living room can be redecorating simply by changing the color of the walls, sofa pillows, drapes or blinds, and slip covers. Wooden tables or other furniture can be stained the same color. On the floor hardwood stands up longer than carpets. Use hardwood or ceramic tile and two inexpensive throw rugs that imitate in design the more expensive oriental rugs.

Match any throw rugs on the floor to the tapestries on the walls if you use wall tapestries. They harbor dust and insects. So you might want to paint murals on the walls using stencils.

What you probably need most are new faucets in the kitchen and bath or new sinks if your basins are cracked. Accessorize. If you don't like your old color scheme, put new colors over your old furniture. It's easier to sew slip covers than to buy a new sofa as long as the basic framework is holding up and there are no tears to the fabric.

The inexpensive quilts you find in discount stores for a queen or king size bed make excellent slip cover throws on sofas. Use a queen size for a love seat and king size for larger sofas. Pick the color scheme you want. Use the pillow slips that come with the quilts to put on your arm rests or sofa pillow throws in matching colors.

14

Draining Duties

Baking soda and vinegar drain cleaner

Make more environmentally-safe cleaning mixes. Add a quarter cup of white, distilled vinegar to your laundry in the rinse water. It won't leave an odor. And it will help to soften the laundry water, dissolve the minerals, and give your clothes that soft, fresh feel so you won't need a commercial fabric softener.

Use multi-purpose cleaners that you can make from *simple, less hazardous* household products such as white distilled vinegar and baking soda. Not only can you live on less expense when you work with basic ingredients such as baking soda and vinegar (drain freshener) or *olive oil and vinegar* (furniture polish), but you'll be using less hazardous substances. See the cleaning recipes at the Web site of the NC State University, College of Agriculture& Life Sciences, and Family & Consumer Sciences Department at: http://www.ces.ncsu.edu/depts/fcs/housing/pubs/fcs3682r.html.

Make your own drain cleaner with baking soda and vinegar. Assemble 1/2 cup baking soda and 1/2 cup white vinegar or any equal parts of baking soda and vinegar if you're working on several drains.

Put a quart of water in a pot or tea kettle and heat it so that you have a pot of boiling water available. First slowly pour the half cup of baking soda down the drain. Add the half cup of white vinegar and cover the drain.

Let the baking soda and vinegar fizz and set for 5 minutes. Then pour a pot of boiling water down the drain. According to the publication, *as a section of publication he-368-2 (January 1991) by Dr. Wilma Hammett, Extension Housing Specialist, North Carolina Cooperative Extension Service, North Carolina State University, Raleigh, NC,* at the NC State University's Web site mentioned above, when you mix vinegar and baking soda, the fizz that occurs is the process of the vinegar and baking soda breaking down fatty acids into soap and glycerin. This process allows the clog to wash down the drain.

Do not use this method if you have used a commercial drain opener and it may still be present in the drain. Remember that you can't use these methods if you have been using chlorine bleach or commercial drain openers that are still in the drain.

Mixing certain products create poisonous and hazardous gasses such as chlorine gas which can be fatal. Do not mix any products if you have a commercial drain cleaner, chlorine, or anything other than water still present in the drain.

See the section on reducing hazardous substances in your home at: http://www.ces.ncsu.edu/depts/fcs/housing/pubs/fcs3682.html.

15

Simple All Purpose Cleaners

To make an all-purpose cleaner, simply mix 4 tablespoons baking soda with 1 quart warm water. Dissolve the baking soda in warm water. Apply with a soft cloth, terry cloth, micro cloth or micro mop or other soft, absorbent cloth or plastic scourer. Don't use a sponge as it drags grime into the grout of ceramic tile. Rinse with clear water. Sponges hold bacteria in their pits and craters. Use a soft cloth that can be cleaned thoroughly. For metal surfaces, such as frying pans, use a plastic scouring pad. For sinks use a soft dish cloth or disposable wiping cloth, or plastic. You don't want to scratch the surfaces.

Furniture Cleaner and Polish

First wipe furniture with a damp washcloth and dry immediately. Then mix two cups of cups olive oil with ½ cup of vinegar. If you have a lot of furniture, mix 3 cups of olive oil with a cup of vinegar. Blend the olive oil and vinegar mixture well. With a soft, dry cloth, apply a small amount of the mixture to wipe your furniture. If you don't like the acidic vinegar eating your furniture, use a small amount of olive oil and wipe dry. Don't use it on your hardwood floor. Instead use black tea and water to shine your hardwood floor. That way, you won't slip on an oily surface.

Lime and Mineral Deposit Remover

Soak disposable wipes or paper towels in distilled white vinegar. Apply the wipes or paper towels to the calcium or lime deposits around the faucet. Leave them on for an hour. The softened deposits can be removed with a few wipes of vinegar and water. To dissolve black or manganese mineral stains, make a paste of cream of tartar and hydrogen peroxide. Let the paste stand on the stain. Then wash the object with water and wipe dry.

Aluminum

Don't use aluminum cookware. It's unhealthy. Aluminum leeches out and ends up in your brain and other organs. It's a toxic metal when it collects inside your organs. Instead use stainless steel cookware. If you have anything that's made of aluminum in your house and want to clean it, mix a quart of water with two tablespoons of cream of tartar. Boil the water and cream of tartar for 10 minutes with the aluminum object in the mixture. If the aluminum object is large, soak paper towels in the boiled water and cream of tartar mixture and apply for an hour, then wipe dry.

Brass Cleaner

There are two ways to clean brass. The first is to mix a little lemon juice, a half-cup for example, with an equal amount of baking soda. Make a paste that looks like toothpaste or wall paper paste. Rub the paste onto brass with a soft cloth. Rinse with water and dry.

The second method is to use lemon juice and cream of tartar. Mix in equal amounts the lemon juice and cream of tartar. Or mix in small amounts until you have the consistency of a paste, such as toothpaste or wallpaper paste. Apply to the brass and let stay for five minutes. Wipe or wash with warm water and dry with a soft cloth that doesn't leave lint.

Stainless Steel Cookware Cleaner

Dip a soft cloth or disposable wipe in undiluted white vinegar. Wipe the surface. You also can use this method to clean chrome such as sink faucets.

Oven Cleaner

Baking soda and water cleans your oven. Buy a large, empty spray bottle in a hardware store and some paper towels or disposable or re-usable wiping cloths. You can use this combination for many purposes.

Fill the spray bottle with water and spray your oven. Then take some baking soda and a plastic scouring pad. Scour gently in circles. Wipe off the grime with the paper towels or re-usable or disposable wipes. Give another spray with the water bottle and then wipe dry.

For really stubborn stains, sprinkle table salt inside a warm oven. When it cools, scrape off the salt that now has absorbed the grime. Then wash the area with water and baking soda or plain water and wipe dry.

Less Toxic Toilet Bowl Cleaners

Pour a cup of baking soda into the toilet bowl. Add a cup of vinegar. After the fizzing stops, scour the bowl with a toilet brush or toilet wand. Another method that uses borax, which is a toxic ingredient, works on tougher toilet stains.

Be careful where you store the borax so no animal or child can reach it, and handle it carefully. Baking soda is less toxic because small amounts (such as a quarter teaspoon) are used in cooking. Baking soda is the less hazardous ingredient.

Here's the toilet bowl or sink cleaning method using borax. Mix a cup of borax with a half cup of lemon juice or equal parts of borax and lemon juice until you get a paste the consistency of wall paper paste or toothpaste.

Flush the toilet so that the bowl gets coated with a thin film of water. Rub the paste inside the toilet bowl and under the rim. Leave the paste in the toilet for two hours. Then scrub and flush.

Chlorine bleach dulls porcelain enamel surfaces when left standing a long time. So don't let it stand in your toilet. It's also a toxic substance. Make more use of common household products such as lemon juice, vinegar, and baking soda.

16

Removing Mineral Deposits and Rust with Cream of Tartar

Use white vinegar and baking soda mixed to form a paste for dissolving soap scum and hard water marks. It certainly beats sniffing the odor of many commercial products for cleaning showers, tubs, and bathroom sinks. Check out the article, *Removing Mineral Deposits from Household Surfaces* at: http://www.ces.ncsu.edu/depts/fcs/housing/pubs/fcs397.html. According to the publication prepared by Dr. Sandra A. Zaslow, Extension District Director, North Carolina Cooperative Extension Service, North Carolina State University, Raleigh, NC, issued in print by the North Carolina Cooperative Extension Service as publication FCS-397 and WQWM-12 (February 1993), published by North Carolina Cooperative Extension Service North Carolina State University, Raleigh, NC, you can use these techniques for removing a variety of household mineral deposits. View the Web site's "Stains at a Glance" summary.

What I like most about the publications at the university's Web sites are the recipes for making household cleaning products and mineral deposit removers with common household products. Such products normally are used in cooking such as lemon juice, cream of tartar, vinegar, and baking soda. Another surprise is making furniture polish from olive oil.

There also are products mentioned that are definitely not used in cooking such as ammonia or borax. The make it yourself recipes mostly call for less toxic, less hazardous, less expensive, and more environment friendly ingredients. What I liked most about this Web site was the recipes for multi-uses of cream of tartar as a cleaning agent and rust remover.

If your gadget or fixture is covered with mineral deposits or rust and *is not acid resistant*, use *cream of tartar*. It's a mild acid. Cream of tartar may be mixed with water to form a paste **rust** remover. Acids help remove hard water deposits. Some acid cleaners help remove discoloration from aluminum, brass, bronze, and copper. Other acids remove iron rust stains. Commercial toilet bowl cleaners, rust removers, metal cleaners, and kitchen and bath cleaners that remove mineral products usually are acids.

Commercial products may have stronger and more toxic acids. Make your own *milder* acid by using white vinegar. It's about 5 percent acetic acid. White vinegar may remove hard water deposits from glass, rust stains from sinks, and tarnish from brass and copper. Another mild acid is lemon juice.

Lemon juice contains citric acid, which can be used in much the same way as vinegar. However, it's easier to open a plastic jug of white vinegar and pour compared to squeezing a dozen fresh lemons to collect the juice and fill a cup. Unless you have a lemon tree in your backyard, the cost of lemons is a price to consider. What if you have pitted surfaces from abrasive cleaners, and you need to remove the rust?

Make a paste of borax and lemon juice. After the paste dries, rinse with water. For really stubborn rust, make a paste of mild scouring powder, cream of tartar, and peroxide. Let it set for 1/2 hour, and then rinse.

To get rid of copper stains (blue-green stains from acidic water) use a mixture of equal parts of water and ammonia. Ventilate the room. Mix a cup of water with a cup of ammonia. Be careful of those caustic fumes. Wear goggles and gloves.

Let the mixture stand on the stained area or wipe after the stains soften. Then rinse and flush pipes with water. Always flush pipes after using anything containing ammonia.

For black stains from manganese and a variety of other minerals, make a paste of cream of tartar and hydrogen peroxide. Let the mixture stand on the object, and then rinse thoroughly. For construction, maintenance, and repair solutions, the North Carolina State University's Web site at http://www.ces.ncsu.edu/depts/fcs/housing/repair.html offers excellent techniques. Check out their index to publications on the Web at: http://www.ces.ncsu.edu/depts/fcs/housing/index.html on these how-to subjects and links.

17

Wood Moisture, Decay, and Mold

Is wood moisture causing allergies, toxic mold, or other damage problems in your house or apartment? Take wood moisture readings. See the North Carolina State University's site at http://www.ces.ncsu.edu/depts/fcs/housing/pubs/fcs486.html for tips on how to take wood moisture readings. At that Web site you'll see their publication called *Moisture Control and Prevention Guide.*

Buy a moisture meter at your local hardware or home improvement center. Insert the probes into the wood and read the indicator. It will tell you the percent of moisture in the surface. Take readings from every corner of a crawl space and the damp areas around plumbing fixtures in kitchens, laundry rooms, garages, and bathrooms. Take readings around the sills under sliding glass doors. Also get readings from places where chimneys, porches, garages, and patios attach to the house.

If you use a pest control firm, ask them to take moisture readings and stay round so you can get a copy of the recordings and watch how they do it so you can do it yourself periodically.

In addition to the toxic mold that grows on wood, fungi will only decay wood with moisture content above the fiber saturation point, which is 30 percent by weight for most species used in construction, according to the NC State University's publication at the Web site mentioned above.

They publication also states that wood with a moisture content of 20 percent and above is susceptible to decay. Make sure the moisture readings of wood in your home or apartment are below the fungi, decay, or mold levels.

Learn how to check for moisture levels before your wood decays or becomes moldy, infested, decayed, and toxic. Think about other products made from wood such as paper and cardboard. Cardboard and paper stored in closets and garages draw insects and mice that feed on paper. Store in plastic containers or jars, not in cardboard and paper. Make sure your books and paper documents are not subject to moisture or light or in open areas where bugs and worms can eat the paper or glue. Book or display cases need doors to protect the objects from dust, sunlight, moisture, acid, and mites.

18

Earning

What can you do to earn money in a hurry and be proud of it— if you don't have a job? Your first step, assuming you have no capital to start with is to provide a service. You can provide a wide variety of services from recording the highlights of people's lives on video and making copies on DVDs as gifts and greetings. Or you could become a secret shopper. Check out the mystery shopper information Web sites, such as the one at Volition.com ® at: http://www.volition.com/mystery.html.

Secret shoppers visit businesses posing as customers. They evaluate the services received and complete an evaluation form. Entrepreneurs use comparative shopping reports to insure that their employees are practicing appropriate selling techniques and providing quality service to customers.

If you want to be a comparison or secret shopper, check out the many Web sites that offer to pay you to shop for them or their clients. Never send any money to anyone for information.

Use the key word "mystery shoppers" to find a listing of these firms on the Web. Visit sites for information only from reputable companies. Make sure you don't sign any agreement where there is an obligation or cost. You can research both USA and international firms. After you check out national or international companies based on their reputation, ask secret shoppers who already work for them to evaluate the company before you sign up.

When you have a credible list of national and international firms, you can sign up as long as there's no clause in the contract that keeps you from leaving without any cost to you. They companies with which you sign on will eventually contact you when they have a store in your area.

Check out the Mystery Shopping Bulletin Board and USA Mystery Shopping Companies List at http://www.volition.com/mysteryUSA1.html. Look at the International Companies Shopping Companies List at: http://www.volition.com/mysteryint.html. ON these and other bulletin boards companies post immediate needs. There's also information regarding what companies other shoppers have used. View the information on who pays on time and who does not. Checking the Web sites for up-to-date information is an excellent way to learn from those who are already secret shoppers.

Comparison shopping can be done for the media or when you write a column on retailing advice. Look at the lists for Canada, Australia, New Zealand and other areas such as Taiwan, Puerto Rico, Guam, Hong Kong, and Japan by clicking on the International Companies List. If you don't like comparison shopping by driving to various stores, try online comparative shopping where you can sit at home and order online using your computer and Internet connection.

You could make money starting bartering clubs or joining one. The idea is to swap goods that you can keep or sell with online sites. Most barter clubs let you swap products rather than pay for them in cash. You can check out the barter clubs to join.

National barter clubs have not done well. Locally, barter clubs do work when people can look over the merchandise in their neighborhood rather than send anything unseen through the mail far away.

Membership fees to barter clubs can run in the hundreds of dollars. Then there are the commissions per trade of up to 15 percent. Some commissions are still only five percent. Other clubs charge a monthly fee, perhaps $20. So the idea of working with someone else's barter club is not exactly living with fewer expenses.

You can start your own local club. Instead of trading products, trade your time. Help someone on a per hour basis, such as tutoring, mentoring, cleaning, sorting, organizing, indexing, editing, speaking, writing, watching, or coaching. You could offer services house sitting or watching and waiting for delivery or construction crews.

Exchange your time for someone else's time. Anything from beauty treatments to cooking lessons can be exchanged. Research the type of credit given or what is given in return for your time and services. Watch out. Barter credit runs out of time. You don't want to lose any opportunity to earn cash for your time rather than spend time and get in return something you don't really need like more knick-knacks to clutter or small living area.

19

Barter

DESCRIPTION OF BUSINESS

Barter consists of trading products and services for other products and services of equal value. You can provide centralized accounting systems, national computer and video networks, comprehensive sales and marketing programs, and comprehensive training for all barter dealers on your videos, in essence creating an exchange of barter dealers.

You would pay members interest on positive balances, sign up new clients for cash income, receive cash income on each trade transaction and on every account you sign, and charge your members a one-time dealer's fee on a per-client basis.

INCOME POTENTIAL

Charge each owner of a barter-exchange business an annual membership fee of $300 to $2,000, with an additional fee paid in trade credits. You can market your barter and trade videos to your club members at a discount, offer events, seminars, conferences, or other networking opportunities to market your videos live, and continue to market videos through mail orders to members and also to the public at large.

Advertise your videos in bartering newspapers, entrepreneurial publications, and in shopping-type newsletters and newspapers which use lots of classified ads. Your income depends on people who want to trade services, products, and property. Make use of direct mail videos with advertising on the videos of products to barter or trade.

Use your video camera to create video ads. You can add electronic mail with your computer or interactive multimedia shopping services to members and/or subscribers for a fee plus a 15 to 20 percent profit margin for yourself.

BEST LOCALE TO OPERATE THE BUSINESS

You can market your barter videos anywhere, but there is special appeal to people in rural areas and small towns or overseas, especially if you want to tap the import/export market. People can barter products from any location, anywhere in the world.

Many people would love to see a barter/trade video to exchange houses for the summer or winter with someone in a far-away country. With the interior of the house and surrounding town on video, easy vacation home bartering can be arranged. People buy what they can see on video first.

TRAINING REQUIRED

Interview the key people who run reputable barter associations. Prepare a list of questions. From the answers that explain step-by-step procedures, learn how to bring the people together with products that are in demand for barter. Study the barter magazines to see what products would have barter appeal. You also can re-sell online what you receive by bartering locally.

Study how the business brokers handle their business sales and propositions. Contact your local Small Business Association, SCORE. The retired executives in SCORE are available to advise you how to startup your new business and give you the benefits of their lifelong experience running businesses. Choose someone from SCORE who has had video experience or bartering trade experience.

GENERAL APTITUDE OR EXPERIENCE

You need patience, an artistic flair, good camera skills, and an interest in business and bartering of products and services of fair and equal value. Experience in bartering or trading goods helps, but all can be learned on the job. Begin small at first with one barter/trade video tape. Form your barter video club first and see how many people join and how fast membership grows. Get feedback from your customers on what they expect.

VIDEO EQUIPMENT NEEDED

You need a camcorder for recording interviews or making instructional videos, lighting and editing equipment, and people to record who have products or services to barter or trade. You also can hook your video camera and VCR player into your personal computer with a FireWire or other video cable that connects your camcorder to your DVD recorder/player and computer. You need a computer printer and broadband or modem to network with other businesses. The estimated cost is $2,500 to $3,500.

Besides tapes and your camera, you need a good word-processing program, a spread-sheet accounting program, blank disks for writing your barter newsletter or enough tape for creating a monthly video newsletter, or less expensive, an electronic mail newsletter about your barter videos, sales reports, fliers, and paper supplies. You can discuss trade and bartering on video or even begin to barter special niche videos with other video collectors. The estimated cost for computer software, tapes, and paperwork office supplies is $800 to $1,000.

OPERATING YOUR BUSINESS:

Your computer can maintain files of your new video-advertising barter and trade club members who represent the largest single source of professional expertise in the financial, legal, and economic aspects of bartering in the world. Members of your trade exchange would be entrepreneurs who cooperate in bartering—either bartering videos on any high-demand topic, or bartering and trading any product or service from real estate to independent contracting. You can also put video ads on tape to barter, trade, or sell anything from garage sale items to recycling appliances, homes, apartment rentals, cars, or anything else.

You could also conduct studies and surveys on barter around the world, using your computer to generate reports and publications that monitor the barter industry. Currently over 130 trade exchanges are members of the International Association of Trade Exchanges.

Many barterers are starting franchises of their barter services. Such franchises must be registered with their state authorities in accordance with the state's franchising laws. Bartering franchises must also demonstrate that they're in compliance with the Federal Trade Commission trade franchising regulations.

Ask members of your barter exchange to submit franchise disclosure statements and organizational documents to your exchange for review. Use your video camera to generate evaluations, to give advice to the public, and to answer questions on how to enter the bartering business.

TARGET MARKET:

Form a video bartering club. Your members can be owners of bartering businesses and franchises or people who are interested in bartering and trading any product, service, or property—from apartment houses to occupational services in exchange for a car or boat.

There are more than two hundred trade exchanges in the United States owned by independent business persons. To reach owners of bartering businesses, write to the International Association of Trade Exchanges, 2948 University Terrace

NW, Washington, DC 20016. Or start your own association of bartering business entrepreneurs to whom you can market bartering videos.

RELATED VIDEO OPPORTUNITIES:
Related to creating bartering/trade videos, is the art of putting business case histories on video. You can combine the two in one service. Corporate video biographies can be made by dealing with businesses and entrepreneurs. Also, you can create shopping videos for garage sales and later go electronic into multimedia, offering interactive shopping videos on computer software.

ADDITIONAL INFORMATION:
International Association of Trade Exchanges,
2948 University Terrace NW,
Washington, DC 20016

American Video Association
557 East Juanita
Mesa, AZ 85204
(602) 892-8553

Mail Advertising Service Association International
7315 Wisconsin Ave, Suite 440-W
Bethesda, MD 20814
(301)654-6272

Direct Marketing Computer Association
60 East 42nd St.
New York, NY 10165
(212) 867-2290

Do-It-Yourself Research Institute
770 North High School Road
Indianapolis, IN 46224
(317) 241-1070

Institute of Certified Professional Business Consultants
221 N. La Salle St.
Suite 2026

Chicago, Il 60601
(312) 346-1600

Bureau of Wholesale Sales Representatives
1819 Peachtree Road NE
Atlanta, GA 30309
(404) 355-3012

Professional and Technical Consultants Association
1190 Lincoln Ave
San Jose, CA 95125
(408) 287-8703

National Business League
4324 Georgia Ave NW
Washington, DC 20011
(202) 829-5900

Institute of Business Appraisers
PO Box 1447
Boynton Beach, FL 33435
(305) 433-0908

International Association of Merger and Acquisitions Consultants
11258 Goodnight Lane
Dallas, TX 75229
(214) 241-0254

20

Opinion Surveys

Your opinions are worth pay. Check out the Web site at http://www.fieldwork. com. How the process works in getting paid for your opinion is that marketing research firms are the companies to apply to for work. The marketing firms form focus groups that research what consumers think and feel about individual products. A typical payment is $100 for a few hours of your time spent filling out forms or answering questions about using the product in a group meeting.

Make money from your opinions. Apply to firms that pay cash. Some pay only in coupons. Coupons are fine when you want to buy a product at a discount, but cash pays bills. Careful, your name and address may end up on endless lists to receive unsolicited junk mail. Then again, you may receive coupons.

You make the decision. If you supply a post office box number, the junk mail or sales material may come to that address instead of flooding your home. Not all companies sell your address to lists, but some may.

That's why it's best not to put personal information such as a social security number into any application. What you fill out may end up on hundreds of lists of addresses to send junk mail to—that is unsolicited mail asking you to buy something or donate money.

Post office boxes can direct mail to the box and not to your home. Never give out your home phone if there's a chance the marketing company might sell your name to another list. Instead use an answering service or a special email address to see to how many lists your name is sold.

Several years ago I was paid $50 for my opinion for using two competing products for a week and then answering questions and filling out forms regarding what I thought about different aspects of each product. Your local phone directly has a category titled "Market Research." Contact all the market research firms in your area and tell them you want paid work for offering your opinion or evaluation of products by using them comparatively.

Another way of generating income in a hurry is to be paid for your opinions by answering *online surveys*. Check out the site at: http://www.volition.com/opinions.html. Some companies pay you only by entering you in sweepstakes for answering their opinion surveys.

When you need cash in a hurry, only look for companies that actually pay you in cash right after you answer their surveys. Try companies such as American Consumer Opinion ®. Their Web site is at: http://www.acop.com/. Most survey companies pay a small amount for your opinion. Some companies require you to be selected before you are paid. So check out the companies online before you spend time filling out opinion surveys.

Another way to earn money quickly is to sell what you have around the house on eBay auctions. Sell used DVDs (documentaries only of interest to teachers and students), old textbooks, used books, audio books, software, and remnants of new fabric with unusual historic designs, (for quilters or costumers) and classical music or multi-ethnic dance music CDs from the world music dance genre. To place an item for auction, look at the instructions on eBay at http://www.eBay.com.

Another way to make money is to put love letters on CDs or DVDs and send them as greeting cards for clients who want the perfect poem or letter send with a slide show, video clips, or public domain music clips in the background.

You can buy reasonably-priced software with public domain music, clip art, and add your own photos, text, or video and audio clips to create love letters or gifts for any reason from graduations and grand openings of stores to rites of passage, eulogies, and wedding greetings or anniversaries. Create multimedia tributes and greetings on DVDs or CDs and mail them for your clients. Charge what the market will bear for these multimedia services. This is one way to market poetry in motion through sound, music, imagery, and text. You can also save Web sites to DVDs for clients.

You can earn money in a hurry by recording family reunion videos. Contact genealogists and groups online for various family surnames. Ask whether they would like an event set up with a DVD time capsule recorded. Use your camcorder to record these meetings. As a family history event planner and videographer, it would be fun to bring people together and produce time capsules such as DVDs of family reunions. This enterprise would combine skills in event planning with an interest in genealogy or history.

Everyone has an interest that could be developed into a skill in which you package and sell information, facts, recorded life stories, history, or events. Some people's interests focus on the how-to step-by-step variety that others can follow.

Other people like to deal with intangible ideas. Facts and ideas as well as step-by-step instruction can be researched and recorded on video and audio.

You can make time capsules or reunions and present events to celebrate a historic event and a person. Or disseminate information to those who want to know more local history, genealogy, or learn specific skills. An event also can be about any subject. You can plan an event for people to meet more people with similar interests and goals.

Decide what categories of people or ages you want to emphasize, what type of special interest groups, and list your plan of events, speakers, or other contacts.

An example would be to plan a special interest group that meets in community centers, schools, churches, or convention centers.

You can offer a service to convention attendees by providing a service such as child care or pet sitting, or finding rooms to rent in private homes for people who attend business conventions in various cities.

List the services needed in your local area. Would you like to help match seniors to share homes, provide child or pet care services to shoppers or travelers, or shop and locate items for individuals or corporations, provide company gift baskets, or write instructional how-to booklets to provide a needed skill in your community? Match your special interests with the need in your area.

The quickest way to make money is to find something to sell that someone else wants and advertise it online. Look into drop-ship services, where without any investment on your part, you can have products delivered directly to someone who buys a product you offer to sell online, for example, on eBay or other online sites set up for people to sell items.

Would you like to become a print-on-demand publisher one book at a time? You need to write a contract first that you'd send to prospective clients. What can you do with that novel that you can't sell to a publisher after four decades of trying?

You can use your computer to offer a service for a small fee. Advertise that you'll write a novel using the name of the person you sell to as the hero character. As long as the person sends a written letter of permission and pays a small fee, all you have to do is insert the person's name on the cover and substitute that person's name for your hero character. Make sure the novel shows the person as likeable and reputable, something the owner will be proud to show to friends.

Your computer's software would substitute any name with the find and replace word menu. You can send the same novel to many people as long as you keep changing the name of the hero and have their permission. Print up the book as a print on demand publication using print on demand software.

You can type set the book as a PDF file. Offer the book either as an e-book or printed as a paperback with nicely designed cover using your graphic design or photo imaging software, (for example, Adobe PhotoShop).

Your client would have a nice paperback book with his or her photo on the cover or any other design emailed to you for the cover or one you select for yourself. Always obtain written permission to use anyone's name.

Charge a fee covering your expenses so you make a small profit on each book. Create any type of book using an individual's name with written permission and send copies of the book as a print-on-demand paperback.

Each book would be typeset as a PDF file, printed and mailed to your client. You can study how a large print-on-demand publisher does it for hundreds of books per month by looking at the Web sites of several publishers. One example would be iUniverse, Inc. at http://www.iUniverse.com. Click on their bookstore and browse. Look at the company's contracts as a guide to writing a contract for your own business, should you desire to print anyone's manuscript as a print-on-demand publication. Compare the contracts of several different print-on-demand publishers online. Then write a business plan of how many books you might like to handle at one time. You might try this with your own book and see whether anything sells.

You'd have to work out a deal with distributors such as Ingram or other large, national book distributors to make sure your published book appeared in books-in-print. People should be able to order the book by walking into a local bookstore.

Many people ask to see a book listed in various books in print online or listed in the actual books in print publications. Not everyone is online. Bookstore clerks usually look online to find the book listed in the distributor's books in print publication. Ask in bookstores which distributors the bookstores use in your area.

Not everyone is interested in disseminating information. Some people like to build projects such as making palaces for cats out of doll houses. Others like to sew items such as quilts or cushiony igloos for cats or build dog houses or other pet-centric items to sell at pet fairs or offer to stores.

If you like to make gift items rather than distribute information in unique ways, then focus on researching your special interest, skills, or learning goals. You can also cater to the needs of various age groups such as new parents or empty nesters, or parents of home-schooled children and teens regarding their learning resources.

What do people need that you can supply at little cost to you? As an example, I review audio books for a national magazine. Make a list of what you would like to do to earn money in unique ways that bring not only income but contacts who also can be your sources of feedback. Use this feedback to develop better skills and services.

21

Empty Nesters

Check out the statistics on Baby Boomers and Empty Nesters at the Escape-Homes.com Web site at: http://www.escapehomes.com/articles/Baby_Boomers_Statistics_on_Empty_Nests_and_Retirement.htm. According to the 2004 Del Webb Baby Boomer Survey, getting out of debt are the Baby Boomers' first priority as empty nesters. When empty nesters that also are Baby Boomers (or beyond) want to live on less and earn more, what the Boomers actually are feeling, according to the 2004 Del Webb Baby Boomer Survey, is an increase in freedom to be themselves.

The survey notes that 75 percent of Boomers don't miss the parenting roles, such as being soccer moms or tutoring school work. However, 64 percent of Boomers do miss the family vacations.

Forty percent of Boomers believe their children will be better off financially than they are. Only 2 percent say they wished they would not have had children. 46 percent would advise future parents to spend less time at work and more time with their children. And 74 percent say they have been good role models.

Twenty-seven percent would not let their grown children move back in with them assuming that their children were in good health and financially secure. Forty percent of Boomers anticipate that their adult children will move back in with them.

Thirty percent anticipate that their parents will move in with them. Do Boomers charge their children rent and their parents rent? Actually, the study noted that 28 percent of Boomers would charge their kids rent, but only eight percent of Boomers would bill their parents who move in with them for rent and/or food.

What if you are a Baby Boomer, an empty nester with adult children? You've paid for their education with your retirement money. Now you decide to travel around the world or across the country to relax and enjoy.

You've spent your life helping your children grow up, graduate from college or trade school, marry, and have their own children. Your goal focused on helping your children to become employable, friendly, and financially responsible.

Your parents live in another city. Suddenly, your parents retire from paid income. Because of health problems, they can't take care of themselves. They can't afford long term care insurance. They sell their home to make ends meet. Declines in investments take away your parents' savings.

At the same time, your children move back in with you with their children. Your daughter becomes pregnant and loses her job.

Your son has health or emotional problems that keep him from working, or he can't find a new job. Now your parents move back in with you taking your son's room. Your children move back in with you taking your daughter's room.

Your grandchildren occupy a spare room. You're about to take your first trip around the world as an empty nester. Do you tell your children, grandchildren, and parents to move in and house sit while you board the cruise ship with your spouse?

Of course you do. It's your turn now. If you wait to become dependent and penniless, will you really have the chance to travel? The message is to list your priorities, plan, and live each day at a time while looking ahead to the future.

Empty nesters who want to live on less should consider putting their parents and adult children to work for them either house sitting while they travel or in a family business that allows each family member to work together in a cottage industry at home doing what they do best—where their natural talents take them. What do you want to do for the long term that you can live on and at the same time promotes your general health?

For example, parents can watch the property. Adult children can work at telecommuting, and grandchildren can do promotional such as voice over work in commercials or help illustrate children's story books. There's a creative endeavor for those who insist they don't have a creative bone in their bodies.

The whole idea is to encourage people to reach their maximum potential by working together as a family unit on living the positive attitude by being of service to others or working on creative expression projects that fill a need in the community.

How can you make working together as an empty nester a step-by-step how to useful skill to share with others? From publishing print-on-demand genealogy research booklets to making time capsules, there's a place for everyone with every type of skill. For the number counters, there are budgeting, planning, and logistics. For the artists, creative projects to expand, and for the people-oriented members, bringing more people together through event planning and budgeting.

22

Energizing Enterprises

What type of enterprise can you start that would enable you to live on fewer expenses? The human genome is a current issue in the news. The topic is popular with visual anthropology videos and is approachable by historians and genealogists as well as the traditional geneticists. DNA reporting picks up where written genealogy records stop.

There are hundreds of businesses you can open with very little capital. You could take drop-ship products from a company at no cost to you. You could sell the products online, on eBay, for example. The products are stored in the company's warehouse, not in your home. You could have the company mail the product directly to the customer after you collect the payment, take your share or commission, and notify the company of the sale and customer's shipping address.

You could offer personal services such as mystery and comparative shopping or personal location services. You could use your family camcorder to record the significant events and personal histories of others and put the stories on DVDs or CDs.

You could house sit, pet sit, offer companionship to people with less mobility, or take people on cultural tours of your favorite places and go free if you gather enough to take the tour. What can you do at home with your computer besides write letters or type manuscripts? You could sell audio books and videos online or write reviews of audio books for magazines.

Place and watch advertisements at online auctions for other people or companies if you had nothing to sell. Your business would be a type of sales assistant who takes care of business for others who have lots of items to sell online and little time to watch when an item is sold or whether questions are asked. Mail packages for people who have sold an item online.

*Start a reporting service. Create **press kits** containing DNA-driven ancestry reports. Create folder-type press kits as well as electronic media kits. Mail the paper press kits with reports to clients who have had their DNA tested for ancestry. Or make* *time capsules on genealogy, ancestry, family history, and DNA testing reports for ancestry.*

With very little capital, you can write a business plan to start *a reporting* service that brings business and client together. One of the easiest enterprises to start with only your computer, printer, and Internet connection is a DNA-driven genealogy reporting service.

You wouldn't have to spend money on equipment such as gifts for gift baskets or fabric, cameras, or other investments. With only your computer, printer, paper, press kit folders, DVD/CD recorder, DVDs and CDs, and email, you can offer information packaged in unique ways. Instead only offering administrative assistant services, typing, or editing and proofreading, you can offer DNA reporting presented in a media kit or package-type folder.

23

How to Open Your Own DNA Test Results or Molecular Genealogy Reporting Company

Did you ever wonder what the next money-making step for entrepreneurs in genealogy is-searching records for family history and ancestry? It's about opening a genealogy-driven DNA testing service. Take your pick: tracking ancestry by DNA for pets or people. You don't need any science courses or degrees to start or operate this small business. It can be done online, at home, or in an office. What should you charge per test? About $200 is affordable. You'll have to pay a laboratory to do the testing. Work out your budget with the laboratory.

Laboratories that do the testing can take up to fifty percent of what you make on each test unless they have research grants to test a particular ethnic group and need donors to give DNA for testing. Each lab is different. Shop around for an affordable, reputable laboratory. Your first step would be to ask the genetics and/ or molecular anthropology departments of universities who's applying for a grant to do DNA testing. Also check out the oral history libraries which usually are based at universities and ethnic museums. You're bringing together two different groups-genealogists and geneticists.

You'd work with the laboratories that do the testing. Customers want to see online message boards to discuss their DNA test results and find people whose DNA sequences match their own.

So you'd need a Web site with databases of the customers, message boards, and any type of interactive communication system that allows privacy and communication. DNA database material would not show real names or identify the people. So you'd use numbers. Those who want to contact others could use regular email addresses. People want ethnic privacy, but at the same time love to find DNA matches. At this point you might want to work only with dogs, horses, or other pets or farm animals providing a DNA testing service for ancestry or nutrition.

Take your choice as an entrepreneur: sending the DNA of people to laboratories to be tested for ancestry or having the DNA of dogs, horses or other pets and animals sent out to be tested for ancestry and supplying reports to owners regarding ancestry or for information on how to tailor food to the genetic signatures of people or animals. For animals, you'd contact breeders.

For people, your next step is to contact genealogists and genealogy online and print publications. You'd focus on specific ethnic groups as a niche market. The major groups interested in ancestry using DNA testing include Northern European, Ashkenazi, Italian, Greek, Armenian, Eastern European, African, Asian, Latin American, and Middle Eastern.

Many successful entrepreneurs in the DNA testing for ancestry businesses started with a hobby of looking up family history records-genealogy. So if you're a history buff, or if your hobby is family history research, oral history, archaeology, or genealogy, you now can turn to DNA testing.

What you actually sell to customers are DNA test kits and DNA test reports. To promote your business, offer free access to your Web site database with all your clients listed by important DNA sequences. Keep names private and use only assigned numbers or letters to protect the privacy of your clients. Never give private and confidential genetic test information to insurance companies or employers. Clients who want to have their DNA tested for ancestry do not want their names and DNA stored to fall into the "wrong hands." So honor privacy requests. Some people will actually ask you to store DNA for future generations.

If you want to include this service, offer a time capsule. For your clients, you would create a time capsule, which is like a secure scrap book on acid-free paper and on technology that can be transferred in the future when technology changes. Don't store anything on materials that can't be transferred from one technology to another. For example, have reports on acid-free paper.

You can include a CD or DVD also, but make sure that in the future when the CD players aren't around any longer, the well-preserved report, perhaps laminated or on vellum or other acid-free materials that don't crumble with age can be put into the time capsule. You can include a scrap book with family photos and video on a CD if you wish, or simply offer the DNA test report and comments explaining to the customer what the DNA shows.

Use plain language and no technical terms unless you define them on the same page. Your goal is to help people find other people who match DNA sequences and to use this knowledge to send your customers reports. If no matches can be found, then supply your clients with a thorough report. Keep out any confusing jargon. Show with illustrations how your customer's DNA was tested. In plain language tell them what was done.

Your report will show the results, and tell simply what the results mean. You can offer clients a list of how many people in what countries have their same DNA sequences. Include the present day city or town and the geographic location using longitude and latitude.

For example, when I had my mtDNA (maternal lineages) tested, the report included my DNA matches by geographic coordinates. The geographic center is 48.30N 4.65E, Bar sur Aube, France with a deviation of 669.62 miles as done by "Roots for Real," a London company that tests DNA for ancestry. The exact sequences are in the Roots for Real Database (and other mtDNA databases) for my markers.

Later, with Family Tree DNA, my mtDNA H1b haplogroup came with a report of possible areas of origin. Maps of the possible geographic origin at different periods of time in prehistory expanded the report. Charts and articles explained the prehistory of how the mtDNA migrated and expanded at the end of the Ice Age. Paragraphs explained where the mtDNA (female lineage) might have originated and where it is found today.

There were charts, maps, and tables tracing the migrations of the mtDNA as it expanded from prehistoric refuges in the Pyrenees to where it is found today on the East coast of the Baltic Sea. The colorful report came in a press kit type folder.

Another company that I highly recommend and have done business with is AncestryByDNA. The company sent me a CD with my report, a colorful folder, and boxed appropriately with images of maps on the box. There were certificates with the DNA haplogroup printed along with my name. AncestryByDNA at: https://www.ancestrybydna.com/default.asp also did a racial percentages test and gave me a certificate with the results printed in graphs and text.

You're going to ask, with no science background yourself, how will you know what to put in the report? That's the second step. You contact a university laboratory that does DNA testing for outside companies. They will generate all the reports for you. What you do with the report is to promote it by making it look visually appealing. Define any words you think the customer won't understand with simpler words that fully explain what the DNA sequences mean and what the various letters and numbers mean. Any dictionary of genetic terms will give you the meaning in one sentence using plain language. Use short sentences in your reports and plain language.

Your new service targets genealogists who help their own customers find lost relatives. Your secondary market is the general public. Most people taking a DNA test for ancestry want information on where their DNA roamed 20,000 years ago and in the last 10,000 years. DNA testing shows people only where their ancient ancestors camped. However, when sequences with other people match exactly, it could point the way to an ancient common ancestor whose descendants went in a straight line from someone with those sequences who lived 10,000 years ago to a common ancestor who lived only a few generations ago.

Those people may or may not actually be related, but they share the same sequences. The relationship could be back in a straight line 20,000 years or more or only a few centuries. Ancient DNA sequences are spread over a huge area, like mine-from Iceland to Bashkortostan in the Urals. DNA sequences that sprung up only a few generations ago generally are limited to a more narrow geographic area, except for those who lived in isolation in one area for thousands of years, such as the Basques.

You would purchase wholesale DNA kits from laboratory suppliers and send the kits to your customer. The customer takes a painless cheek scraping with a felt or cotton type swab or uses mouthwash put into a small container to obtain DNA that can help accurately determine a relationship with either a 99.9% probability of YES or a 100% certainly that no near term relationship existed.

The DNA sample is sealed and mailed to a laboratory address where it is tested. The laboratory then disposes of the DNA after a report is generated. Then you package the report like a gift card portfolio, a time capsule, or other fancy packaging to look like a gift. You add your promotional material and a thorough explanation of what to expect from the DNA test-the results.

The best way to learn this business is to check out on the Web all the businesses that are doing this successfully. Have your own DNA tested and look at the printout or report of the results. Is it thorough? Does it eliminate jargon? Include in the report materials the client would like to see. Make it look like a press kit. For example, you take a folder such as a report folder. On the outside cover print the name of your company printed and a logo or photograph of something related to DNA that won't frighten away the consumer. Simple graphic art such as a map or globe of the world, a prehistoric statue, for example the Willendorf Venus, or some other symbol is appropriate.

Inside, you'd have maps, charts, and locations for the client to look at. Keep the material visual. Include a CD with the DNA sequences if you can. The explanation would show the customer the steps taken to test the DNA.

Keep that visual with charts and graphs. Don't use small print fonts or scientific terminology to any extent so your customer won't feel your report is over his or her head. Instead use illustrations, geographic maps. Put colorful circles on the cities or geographic locations where that person's DNA is found.

Put a bright color or arrow on the possible geographic area of origin for those DNA sequences. Nobody can pinpoint an exact town for certain, but scientists know where certain DNA sequences are found and where they might have sat out the last Ice Age 20,000 years ago, and survived to pass those same DNA sequences on to their direct descendants, that customer of yours who has those sequences.

In the last decade, businesses have opened offering personality profilers. This decade, since the human genome code was cracked and scientists know a lot more about DNA testing for the courtroom, DNA testing businesses have opened to test DNA for information other than who committed a crime or to prove who's innocent.

Applications of DNA testing now are used for finding ancient and not-so-ancient ancestry. DNA testing is not only used for paternity and maternity testing, but for tailoring what you eat to your genetic signature. The new field of pharmacogenetics also tests DNA for markers that allow a client to customize medicine to his or her genetic expression.

Perhaps you're an entrepreneur with no science background. That's your skill as long as your laboratory contacts are reputable scientists. Contact DNA testing laboratories. Show them how you can package their reports. Results could go into folders, press kits, and on CDs. You can make colorful packages of information with explanations, maps, or charts and graphs.

A liaison service for connecting the DNA testing companies to the media is another service, offering electronic press kits. Another service would be to write and package the reports so that genealogists would understand what the DNA reports revealed as pertaining to ancestry where written records are not found.

Your goal would be to explain the report is explained in plain language and visually to their customers. Find out who the various DNA testing companies contract with as far as testing laboratories. For example, Family Tree DNA at the Web site: http://www.familytreedna.com/faq.html#q1 sends its DNA samples to be tested by the DNA testing laboratories at the University of Arizona. I've done business with them several times for family members and with surname groups and also highly recommend them.

Here's an example of one of the DNA testing companies for ancestry that provides extensive reports on their Web site and sends customers their DNA results with explanations in plain language of what the results mean. Bennett Greenspan, President and CEO of Family Tree DNA founded Family Tree in 1999. Greenspan is an entrepreneur and life-long genealogy enthusiast. He successfully turned his family history and ancestry hobby into a full-time vocation running a DNA testing-for-ancestry company.

Together with Max Blankfeld, they founded in 1997 GoCollege.com a website for college-bound students which survived the .COM implosion. Max Blankfeld is Greenspan's Vice President of Operations/Marketing. Before entering the business world, Blankfeld was a journalist. After that, he started and managed several successful ventures in the area of public relations as well as consumer goods both in Brazil and the US. Today, the highly successful Family Tree DNA is America's first genealogy-driven DNA testing service.

At the University of Arizona, top DNA research scientists such as geneticist, Mike Hammer, PhD, population geneticist Bruce Walsh, PhD, geneticist Max F. Rothschild, molecular anthropologist, Theodore G. Schurr, and lab manager, Matthew Kaplan along with the rest of the DNA testing team do the testing and analysis.

So it's important if you want to open your own DNA for ancestry testing company to contract with a reputable laboratory to do the testing. Find out whether the lab you're going to be dealing with will answer a client's questions in case of problems with a test that might require re-testing.

Clients will come to you to answer questions rather than go to the busy laboratory. Most laboratories are either part of a university, a medical school, or are independent DNA testing laboratories run by scientists and their technicians and technologists.

Your business will have a very different focus if you're only dealing with genealogy buffs testing their DNA for ancestry than would a business testing DNA for genetic risk markers in order to tailor a special diet or foods to someone's genetic risk markers. For that more specialized business, you'd have to partner with a nutritionist, scientist, or physician trained in customizing diets to genetic signatures.

Many independent laboratories do test genes for the purpose of tailoring diets to genes. The new field is called nutrigenomics. Check out the various Web sites devoted to nutrigenomics if you're interested in this type of DNA testing business. For example, there is Alpha-Genetics at http:// www.Alpha-Genics.com.

According to Dr. Fredric D. Abramson, PhD, S.M., President and CEO of AlphaGenics, Inc., "The key to using diet to manage genes and health lies in managing gene expression (which we call the Expressitype). Knowing your genotype merely tells you a starting point. Genotype is like knowing where the entrance ramps to an interstate can be found. They are important to know, but tell you absolutely nothing about what direction to travel or how the journey will go. That is why Expressitype must be the focus." You can contact AlphaGenics, Inc. at: http:// www.Alpha-Genics.com or write to: Maryland Technology Incubator, 9700 Great Seneca Highway, Rockville, MD 20850.

Why open any kind of a DNA testing business? It's because the entrepreneur is at the forefront of a revolution in our concept of ancestry, diet, and medicines. Genes are tested to reveal how your body metabolizes medicine as well as food, and genes are tested for ancient ancestry or recent relationships such as paternity. Genes are tested for courtroom evidence.

So you have the choice of opening a DNA testing service focusing on diet, ancestry, skin care product matches, or medicine. You can have scientists contract with you to test genes for risk or relationships. Some companies claim to test DNA in order to determine whether the skin care products are right for your genetic signature. It goes beyond the old allergy tests of the eighties.

"Each of us is a unique organism, and for the first time in human history, genetic research is confirming that one diet is not optimum for everyone," says Abramson. Because your genes differ from someone else's, you process food and supplements in a unique way. Your ancestry is unique also.

Do you want to open a business that tunes nutrition to meet the optimum health needs of each person? If so, you need to contract with scientists to do the testing. If you have no science background, it would be an easier first step to open a business that tests DNA only for ancestry and contract with university laboratories who know about genes and ancestry.

Your client would receive a report on only the ancestry. This means the maternal and/or paternal sequences. For a woman it's the mtDNA that's tested. You're testing the maternal lineages. It's ancient and goes back thousands of years. For the man, you can have a lab test the Y-chromosome, the paternal lineages and the mtDNA, the maternal lineages.

What you supply your clients with is a printout report and explanation of the individual's sequences and mtDNA group called the haplogroup and/or the Y-chromosome ancestral genetic markers. For a male, you can test the Y-chromosome and provide those markers, usually 25 markers and the mtDNA. For a woman, you can only test the mtDNA, the maternal line for haplogroup letter and what is called the HVS-1 and HVS-2 sequences. These sequences show the maternal lineages back thousands of years. To get started, look at the Web sites and databases of all the companies that test for ancestry using DNA.

What most of the DNA testing entrepreneurs have in common is that they can do business online. People order the DNA testing kit online. The companies send out a DNA testing kit. The client sends back DNA to a lab to be tested. The process does not involve any blood drawing to test for ancestry. Then the company sends a report directly to the customer about what the DNA test revealed solely in regard to ancient ancestry-maternal or paternal lines.

Reports include the possible geographic location where the DNA sequences originated. Customers usually want to see the name of an actual town, even though towns didn't exist 10,000 years ago when the sequences might have arisen. The whole genome is not tested, only the few ancestral markers, usually 500 base pairs of genes. Testing DNA for ancestry does not have anything to do with testing genes for health risks because only certain genes are tested-genes related to ancestry. And all the testing is done at a laboratory, not at your online business.

If you're interested in a career in genetics counseling and wish to pursue a graduate degree in genetics counseling, that's another career route. For information, contact The American Board of Genetic Counseling. Sometimes social workers with some coursework in biology take a graduate degree in genetic counseling since it combines counseling skills with training in genetics and in interpreting genetics tests for your clients.

Most people in a hurry to make a living by offering a home-based online service need not think about going to school and spending money with the hope of being hired. Instead, think in terms of providing a unique, inexpensive service to people interested in exploring their ancestry, DNA, nutrition, or genealogy. Think in terms of offering reports and time capsules.

Think of creating heirlooms. Offer genealogy dolls or puppets and personal history videos on DVDs. What new ways can you develop to bring people together joining family history to technology? Think in terms of virtual reunions, event planning, running a speaker's bureau, or giving information and history on media that stands up to the test of time and technology.

Help people trace their female ancestors' through lists of maiden names from hidden sources. You too, can provide services and skills regardless of your training emphasis. The way to tap into creativity is to take a proverb or quotation and expand on it, personalize it, and find your niche in its goal.

Here's one example: *"Destiny is not a matter of chance, it is a matter of choice. It is not a thing to be waited for; it is a thing to be achieved."* (William Jennings). How can you make that proverb your goal and use it to serve others in order to make a living by living with fewer expenses?

Find a way to package and sell new ways to help people make choices and decisions. Develop a list of pros and cons, a plan, and a course or seminar on how to make better choices and decisions. Package it, and offer it to speakers, teachers, and students, as extended studies seminars, courses, and training materials. It can be offered in the form of CDs, DVDs, tapes, books, course syllabi, or live presentations. If you don't like to speak in public, offer your self-published package to speakers' bureaus, convention-panel speakers, and public speakers on the topic of your interest.

Resources for DNA Testing

The American Board of Genetic Counseling.
9650 Rockville Pike
Bethesda, MD 20814-3998
Phone: (301) 571-1825
FAX: (301) 571-1895
http://www.abgc.net/

Below is a list of several DNA-testing companies. Some of these companies test DNA only for ancestry. Other companies listed below test genes for personalized medicine and nutrigenomics, and some companies test for nutrigenomics, pharmacogenetics, and ancestry.

You'll also find several companies listed that only test the DNA of animals. So you have a choice of testing DNA for a variety of purposes, for testing human DNA only, or for testing animal DNA. And the applications for testing genetic signatures are growing, since this science is still in its infancy in regard to applications of genetic and genomic testing.

Roots for Real
http://www.rootsforreal.com
Address: PO Box 43708
London W14 8WG UK

Family Tree DNA—Genealogy by Genetics, Ltd.
World Headquarters
1919 North Loop West, Suite 110 Houston, Texas 77008, USA
Phone: (713) 868-1438 | Fax: (713) 868-4584

info@FamilyTreeDNA.com
http://www.familytreedna.com/

Oxford Ancestors
Oxford Ancestors, London,
http://www.oxfordancestors.com/

AncestrybyDNA, DNAPrint genomics, Inc.
900 Cocoanut Ave, Sarasota, FL 34236. USA
Tel: 941-366-3400 Fax: 941-952-9770
Web site: http://www.ancestrybydna.com/

GeneTree DNA Testing Center
2495 South West Temple
Salt Lake City, UT 84115
Toll Free: (888) 404-GENE
Phone: (801) 461-9757
Fax: (801) 461-9761, http://www.genetree.com/

Trace Genetics LLC
P.O. Box 2010
Davis, California 95617
info@tracegenetics.com
http://www.tracegenetics.com/aboutus.html

Predictive Genomics for Personalized Medicine including Nutrigenomics
AlphaGenics Inc.
9700 Great Seneca Highway
Rockville, Maryland 20850
Email: info@alpha-genics.com
http://www.alpha-genics.com/index.php

Genovations TM
Great Smokies Diagnostic Laboratory/Genovations(tm)
63 Zillicoa Street
Asheville, NC 28801 USA
http://www.genovations.com/

Centre for Human Nutrigenomics
http://www.nutrigenomics.nl/
According to its Web site, "The Centre for Human NutriGenomics aims at establishing an international centre of expertise combining excellent pre-competitive research and high quality (post)graduate training on the interface of genomics, nutrition and human health."

Nutrigenomics Links: http://nutrigene.4t.com/nutrigen.htm

Veterinary DNA Testing

Veterinary Genetics Laboratory
University of California, Davis
One Shields Avenue
Davis, CA 95616-8744
http://www.vgl.ucdavis.edu/

According to their Web site, "The Veterinary Genetics Laboratory is internationally recognized for its expertise in parentage verification and genetic diagnostics for animals. VGL has provided services to breed registries, practitioners, individual owners and breeders since 1955." The Veterinary Genetics Laboratory performs contracted DNA testing.
Alpaca/Llama
Beefalo
Cat
Cattle
Dog
Elk
Goat
Horse
Sheep

DNA Testing of Dogs and Horses:
VetGen, 3728 Plaza Drive, Suite 1, Ann Arbor, Michigan, 48108 USA
http://www.vetgen.com/

Ethnic Genealogy Web Sites

Acadian/Cajun: & French Canadian: http://www.acadian.org/tidbits.html

African-American: http://www.cyndislist.com/african.htm
African Royalty Genealogy: http://www.uq.net.au/~zzhsoszy/
Albanian Research List: http://feefhs.org/al/alrl.html
Armenian Genealogical Society: http://feefhs.org/am/frg-amgs.html
Asia and the Pacific: http://www.cyndislist.com/asia.htm
Austria-Hungary Empire: http://feefhs.org/ah/indexah.html
Baltic-Russian Information Center: http://feefhs.org/blitz/frgblitz.html
Belarusian-Association of the Belarusian Nobility:
http://feefhs.org/by/frg-zbs.html
Bukovina Genealogy: http://feefhs.org/bukovina/bukovina.html
Carpatho-Rusyn Knowledge Base: http://feefhs.org/rusyn/frg-crkb.html
Chinese Genealogy: http://www.chineseroots.com.
Croatia Genealogy Cross Index: http://feefhs.org/cro/indexcro.html
Czechoslovak Genealogical Society Int'l, Inc.:
http://feefhs.org/czs/cgsi/frg-cgsi.html
Eastern Europe: http://www.cyndislist.com/easteuro.htm
Eastern European Genealogical Society, Inc.: http://feefhs.org/ca/frg-eegs.html
Eastern Europe Ethnic, Religious, and National Index with Home Pages include
the FEEFHS Resource Guide that lists organizations associated with FEEFHS
from 14 Countries. It also includes Finnish and Armenian genealogy resources:
http://feefhs.org/ethnic.html
'Ethnic,' 'Religious,' and "National Index"—14 countries:
http://feefhs.org/ethnic.html
Finnish Genealogy Group: http://feefhs.org/misc/frgfinmn.html
Galicia Jewish SIG: http://feefhs.org/jsig/frg-gsig.html
German Genealogical Digest: http://feefhs.org/pub/frg-ggdp.html
Greek Genealogy Sources on the Internet:
http://www-personal.umich.edu/~cgaunt/greece.html
Genealogy Societies Online List:
http://www.daddezio.com/catalog/grkndx04.html
German Research Association: http://feefhs.org/gra/frg-gra.html
Greek Genealogy (Hellenes-Diaspora Greek Genealogy):
http://www.geocities.com/SouthBeach/Cove/4537/
Greek Genealogy Home Page: http://www.daddezio.com/grekgen.html
Greek Genealogy Articles: http://www.daddezio.com/catalog/grkndx01.html
India Genealogy: http://genforum.genealogy.com/india/
India Family Histories:
http://www.mycinnamontoast.com/perl/results.cgi?region=79&sort=n

India-Anglo-Indian/Europeans in India genealogy:
http://members.ozemail.com.au/~clday/
Irish Travelers: http://www.pitt.edu/~alkst3/Traveller.html
Japanese Genealogy: http://www.rootsweb.com/~jpnwgw/
Jewish Genealogy: http://www.jewishgen.org/infofiles/
Latvian Jewish Genealogy Page: http://feefhs.org/jsig/frg-lsig.html
Lebanese Genealogy: http://www.rootsweb.com/~lbnwgw/
Lithuanian American Genealogy Society: http://feefhs.org/frg-lags.html
Melungeon: http://www.geocities.com/Paris/5121/melungeon.htm
Mennonite Heritage Center: http://feefhs.org/men/frg-mhc.html
Middle East Genealogy: http://www.rootsweb.com/~mdeastgw/index.html
Middle East Genealogy by country: http://www.rootsweb.com/~mdeastgw/
index.html#country
Native American: http://www.cyndislist.com/native.htm
Polish Genealogical Society of America: http://feefhs.org/pol/frg-pgsa.html
Quebec and Francophone: http://www.francogene.com/quebec/amerin.html
Romanian American Heritage Center: http://feefhs.org/ro/frg-rahc.html
Slovak World: http://feefhs.org/slovak/frg-sw.html
Slavs, South: Cultural Society: http://feefhs.org/frg-csss.html
Syrian and Lebanese Genealogy: http://www.genealogytoday.com/family/syrian/
Syria Genealogy: http://www.rootsweb.com/~syrwgw/
Tibetan Genealogy:
http://www.distantcousin.com/Links/Ethnic/China/Tibetan.html
Turkish Genealogy Discussion Group:
http://www.turkey.com/forums/forumdisplay.php3?forumid=18
Ukrainian Genealogical and Historical Society of Canada: http://feefhs.org/ca/
frgughsc.html
Unique Peoples: http://www.cyndislist.com/peoples.htm
Note: The Unique People's list includes: Black Dutch, Doukhobors, Gypsy,
Romany, Irish Travelers, Melungeons, Metis, Miscellaneous, and Wends/Sorbs

24

Entertainment

Cut expenses on entertainment by looking for free or low-cost entertainment. Most university campuses offer free concerts where graduate or advanced music students present rehearsals or master's thesis concerts and similar free performances, plays, or lectures open to the public.

With a library card, you can view free educational, business, scientific and literary videos, attend the free days for museums and galleries, and enjoy free concerts given in places such as shopping malls, museums, or library galleries. On the Web, you'll find The FreeBay.com site at: http://www.thefreebay.com/. There is a Freebie site also at: http://www.eversave.com/eversave/consumers/Campaign Reg.jsp?sourceid=7632&cid=163. You can find free coupons and other free offers. You can get ideas about what people buy from sites such as Shop.com at: http://www.shop.com/.

Look for free entertainment by various music bands that come to malls on certain days of the week at certain times, such as a noon lunch hour. Some churches offer free concerts at noon or evenings for downtown works to spend their lunch hour.

Check out FreebieDot.com at the Web site: http://www.freebiedot.com/3p1.htm. Look at FreeMovieMayhem.com at http://www.freemoviemayhem.com/index.cgi?src=WC-31275aaa:33320:

Look at sites such as Memolink.com or FreeDVDs.com at: http://www.freedvds.com/Default.aspx?N=1&P=168. In short, there are freebie sites on the Web. Check them out as to what the conditions are. Free entertainment is available without having to go online. Find out what free entertainment such as music exists at your local college campuses, high schools, churches, public libraries, art galleries, concert halls, museums, and community centers or shopping malls. Public places often have days of the year offering free entertainment or admission.

Make your own free entertainment by visiting parks, museums, church picnics, community centers, galleries and libraries, targeting days with free admissions. If the zoo or museum cost too much to bring your family to frequently, buy a year membership at a discount or volunteer to work there as a docent a few days a year in exchange for a free pass for you and a guest.

Zoos also have one day a year with free admission. To cut expenses, show up early. If there's a particular museum, gallery, or exhibit you want to attend, offer to volunteer there a few days a year in exchange for a free admittance to the exhibit.

Conventions, conferences, meetings, and theatrical presentations also offer free attendance in exchange for volunteer work as an usher or registrar, people-greeter, ticket-taker or other helpful work.

When various theaters present plays and music concerts, they usually need volunteer ushers who get to attend the play or concert free. Call a few weeks in advance and offer to be a volunteer usher, people greeter, helper, or ticket-taker in exchange for getting to attend the particular function.

If you like to attend a lot of plays or, offer to volunteer for university or even high school plays. If you're an older adult, contact various senior centers and theaters and volunteer to give information or help people when the plays or concerts open. You'll get a free admittance in exchange. The same works for art galleries and museums.

If you enjoy hanging around radio or TV stations, call in advance and ask to be put on their volunteer list. Most duties involve answering questions for people who call. Galleries and museums use volunteers as docents. You can do fund-raising work for public TV and radio stations in exchange for free tickets to various functions, such as theatrical or musical productions or live shows.

If you want to work in public relations roles, volunteer to help out at conferences, conventions, or concerts. If you want to become more involved as an event planner, join professional associations for event planners and offer to help find speakers for a panel.

By volunteering, you can learn more about how event planners put together an event or how artists or musicians are promoted.

Another field in the entertainment business is selling the music of professional musicians to the movie industry. You'd be the middle person or go-between finding the right musicians and placing their work with various movie producers and directors.

For those who only want free entertainment without much complexity or involvement in the industry, by volunteering a few days a year in any media, you can ask for free tickets to an event in exchange for being a helper when help is needed. Helpers in the entertainment industry answer phone calls at a radio station or greet and register people at a convention. It's a form of bartering a few hours a year of volunteering in exchange for tickets for you and a guest to attend specific entertainment events.

Not everyone wants an actual career in the entertainment industry You may only want free tickets to see a show or look around in a museum, zoo, or at a convention. Another form of free entertainment is to become an independent tour guide.

You find a required number of persons to pay for a cruise or tour, and you go free on the tour or cruise. Check out the cruise lines and various tours and travel businesses that allow you to go free if you find a required number of paid guests.

Take advantage of free walking tours of various cities. For example at the Web site: http://www.newyorkmetro.com/urban/guides/nyonthecheap/pleasures/walkingtours.htm, you'll find New York metro.com. The site explains that the free walking tours give specific details and history of a neighborhood. Almost every city offers free walking tours. That's another type of free entertainment. To find free walking tours for other cities, just use your Internet's Web search engine and put in the key word "free walking tours." What pops up, for example, at http://www.google.com is a list of Web sites from various cities offering free walking tours.

Look for docent organizations, and consider giving a free walking tour yourself of your city to meet a lot of new people. Become a docent, a volunteer who offers a tour of a place, city, neighborhood, museum or gallery. Join docent groups and receive free training to be a docent. Or just take advantage of the free walking tours of any city. You'll see online free walking tours of various European cities. It's your choice of where you want to take your free walking tour or offer one in your neighborhood.

If you're looking for free entertainment, the walking tour will give you some exercise and outdoors experience. You can choose where you'd like to walk.

An example of docent training and free walking tours would include Las Angelitas in California. If you attend their docent training when it's offered, you can learn about early California and Los Angeles history and how to give small group tours.

After completion, requirements are to give tours 2 weekday mornings per month or 1 Saturday morning. Las Angelitas is a diverse group of people from all over Southern California who also go on historical tours and have social gatherings.

With free entertainment such as walking tours, they are useful if you're interested in history. Most docent groups include social gatherings. It's a good way to make new friends with similar interests and experience the free entertainment.

Historical walking tours can be started in almost any place where people are willing to take walks and discuss the historical events of that community.

Every spot in the world has its own history. And history is as much entertainment as walking. For persons with disabilities, for example, wheelchair historical tours or tours for the deaf community also are resources to help others learn the history of a neighborhood, institution or city. Also try campus walking tours. For example, the University of California, Berkeley has walking tours of the campus where there also are nearby museums. Cultural tours are forms of entertainment where you learn where your values direct you.

Join professional or trade associations and offer to find people to give presentations or speakers for their panels. Whenever an expo, trade show, conference, convention or meeting is scheduled, the professional association or society needs volunteers to help run the show. You get to attend the expo or show free, listen to speakers or enjoy the entertainment.

To find speakers for panels, you contact speakers' bureaus and members of the association with expertise in an area and experience in public speaking. Bring the speaker to the convention and get rewarded with free entertainment. You work through either event planners or the trade association/professional group, or volunteer to work on the group's newsletter.

Another way to work the conventions is to greet people and register newcomers. You can be a ticket-taker or help the event planner. If you're looking for a career as a party-planner, working with event planners is one way to learn the ropes.

Entertainment is a broad area to define. Looking for free entertainment can be found at libraries or theme parks, hotels, casinos, and at performances of musicians or artists at college campuses. A quick way to find out what's free is to call talent agents and promotional companies in advance and ask what you can do to help in exchange for free tickets. Of course, the easiest way is to check with convention and visitor's bureaus and information bureaus for any city and ask what the free admission days are for the local events such as zoos, museums, galleries, theaters, concert halls, and theme parks.

Free university lectures are given almost daily. Check the particular college's newspaper for dates of free lectures. Also check each department's list of events. My field of interest is listening to anthropology lectures. I'd call the department of anthropology at several universities nearby as well as the museums and ask what days free lectures are given that are open to the public.

You'd be surprised at how many people are speaking at university ballrooms and auditoriums, for which most of these lectures are free and open to the public interested in that particular subject. Some people giving an oral presentation for a graduate thesis welcome strangers to quietly sit in the room or auditorium and listen to their presentation to their faculty advisers.

Entertainment that's free can come in the form of seminars. For example, the Federal Technology Center presented a free seminar on negotiation. Business information is a form of entertainment. Contact your local small business and economic development center. Free seminars are frequently offered.

Newspapers that emphasize niche markets such as job listings and information often present career fairs. Attend a free career fair. It usually offers free lectures, seminars, and sometimes entertainment. Attend the free franchise expo circuit. These franchise expos at hotels offer seminars, exhibits, or entertainment, and sometimes free giveaway items such as pens, note pads, samples of products, mugs, book marks, or paperweights.

Make the rounds of exhibits and trade shows. The vendors' rooms are often free to attend. You can also ask a local weekly paper for an assignment to write up the highlights of the convention in exchange for a letter asking for a free press badge.

With a press pass or free press badge, you can attend the lectures and entertainment of the convention or trade show. When you're done, turn in a one-page media release of any important facts you've learned from attending the conference.

Interview the vendors and emphasize what's the upcoming trend and what's most popular on the agenda. Then turn in to the publication your typed two-page story. Or email it.

Ask the editor of any professional association's newsletter if you could review the convention in exchange for a free press pass to the convention. You wouldn't get paid for the article, but you'd get a press pass to attend the convention free. Trade publications, professional associations' newsletters, niche market magazines, such as local computer publications, popular Web sites, and weekly business publications are most likely to be interested.

Attend the job fairs at your local convention center. Usually, there's some form of free entertainment. If you have young children, volunteer at various children's theater projects. Most cities have a children's theater or drama group. If you want to attend expensive business awards banquets, ask whether you can be a volunteer.

Besides the general chamber of commerce groups, there's also the various ethnic chamber of commerce associations that present annual business awards at banquets. Although tickets to these affairs cost upwards of $100, there may be a spot for someone who volunteers to be of help where needed for the event, if you call well in advance.

Most ethnic chambers of commerce include the name of a city followed by the ethnic group such as "Hispanic chamber of commerce" or "African-American Women's chamber of commerce" or "Asian chamber of commerce." How many different ethnic chambers of commerce can you locate?

The smaller the niche, the more opportunity you have to get to work with people in exchange for a free ticket to entertainment offered or a chance to help promote projects, causes, or raise money for the group. You can work with church groups also that offer entertainment in connection with a project.

Look in your area. Call your local college's ethnic studies department. Find out how many different ethnic or other category chambers of commerce in your area are giving business awards and recognition banquets.

Other forms of entertainment can occur in your home. Free CDs or DVDs can be obtained if you volunteer or perform paid work part time as an audio book reviewer. Check out the various audio publishers' associations. Then contact magazines that publish short reviews, usually about 100 to 110 words per review. Offer your reviewing services, and you'll be placed on the publisher's or the publication's list to receive several audio books each month.

In exchange for reviewing the audio book for a publication, you'll receive the books free which you can keep or sell on eBay or other online sales sites or sell at garage sales. Or you can just enjoy the free entertainment and eventually donate your audio CDs or cassettes to libraries, libraries for the blind, or schools where they are needed.

Some publications pay writers to review audio books. You can contact the publishers of the audio books directly or go through magazines that publish reviews. When you've made yourself known as an audio book reviewer, video or DVD reviewer, or print book reviewer, publishers and publications will contact you.

Also, your Web site can be used to practice writing reviews. Keep them one paragraph in length and about 110 words. Emphasize the audio presentation, not the literary review, unless you're reviewing a print book.

Contact authors for "author interviews" in addition to reviews, and offer the interviews to magazines with the approval of the author for a taped interview. Ask the magazine in advance for a go-ahead before you contact the author. Give the author the chance to change anything he or she said before you send out a transcribed and edited tape interview. Keep the number of words to what the publication wants as space is very limited.

25

Inspirational Markets and Experiences

It makes no difference what religion or spirituality essence you select, but writing a life story for the religious or inspirational markets is in demand and expanding its need for sharing life story experience in the form of books, stories, or featured articles and columns.

What the religious or inspirational markets are looking for is sharing what you've learned from your mistakes or experiences, how you arrived at your choices, and how you've grown and were transformed. Your message would be how you gained wisdom that everyone can share.

By sharing your experiences and life story, readers will learn how you made decisions and why, what wisdom you gained from your growth or transformation, and what made it possible for you to grow and change and become a stronger and better person.

The stories you'd write about would be those universal messages we all go through, such as rites of passage, dealing with the stages of life in new ways, finding alternatives, and how you handled the challenges.

The religious and spiritual or inspirational markets want stories that offer pictures and choices and show how you solved your problems. The reason people read your story is to find out how to solve their own problems and make decisions. Give them information they can use to make decisions, even if you write fiction. Have some authority and truth in the fiction, particularly about facts and historical information.

People buy your story to make choices, including choices in the later stages of life or choices in growing up and making transitions. As people move from one career to another or from one stage of life to the next, they want to read about how you made that passage in time and space, and what choices you made.

Life story writing should be more preventive than reactive. Biography writing is reactive because it responds only when people are in need, in transition, or in turmoil. What sells is preventive story writing. Give transformation, growth, and problem solving information so people will be able to prevent making your past mistakes.

Show them how you've learned from your mistakes and pass on your wisdom, growth, and change. Readers want to share your understanding.

Put rewards and possibilities for personal growth into your life story. Don't merely dump your pain and prior abuse on readers or your history of how you were tortured. That's not going to solve their problems. What will is writing about how you've worked at understanding challenges. Look at your readers as your future selves.

Approach life story writing as you would approach writing song lyrics. Pick an industry and focus on the industry as you develop a life story built around an industry or event. If you write about your own life story, do interviews. Gather many different views.

You'll discover blind spots you would never have noticed about yourself. Treat your life story not only as a diary with a one-sided view, but as a biography. Interview many people who have had contact with you as you grew up or during the experience you're targeting.

Writing the Forward

If you write a biography of another person as a book, story or article, or as fiction in a novel, you'll need a foreword. This is what you're doing as you first meet the person you're interviewing. Have two tape recorders going at the same time in case one isn't working properly. Get permission to record. Write what you're doing as you first meet the person you're interviewing. It should be about 16 double-spaced pages or 8 printed pages, or less.

Writing the Preface

What is the person most conscious of? What is the individual whose biography you're writing doing right now as you first interview that person? What's the biography going to zoom in on? Describe the body language.

In Andrew Morton's Monica's Story, Monica stifles a yawn and pulls on black leggings as the preface opens with the title "Betrayal at Pentagon City." The preface summarizes the most important event in the entire biography.

It should be about 10 double-spaced pages or 5 printed pages. Is your character going to be the right person at the right time in the wrong place? Or the wrong person at the wrong time in the right place?

Writing your First Chapter

Begin with the person immediately becoming involved in the action if he is not well-known. If your person is in the news and a known celebrity or royalty, start with the date and season.

It's all right to begin with the birth of your biographical character if the childhood has some relationship to the biography. You can describe the parents of the character if their relationship has a bearing on the life of the main character you're portraying.

The less famous or news-worthy your character, the more you need to start with the character involved in the middle of the action or crisis, the most important event. Avoid any scenes where the book or story opens and the character is in transit flying to some destination. Start after the arrival, when the action pace is fast and eventful.

Characters

You can make a great career writing true story books about people in the news, celebrities, and the famous. If these are the type of books you want to write, focus on the character's difficult childhood if it's important to the story and the character is famous or in the news frequently. To create the tension, get into any betrayals by the third chapter. Show how your character's trusting nature snared the individual in a treacherous web, if that's in your story. If not, highlight your main crisis here in the third chapter.

By the fourth chapter, show the gauntlet or inquiry your character is going through. How did it affect your character and the person's family? How will it haunt your character? Where will your character go from here? What are the person's plans?

Focus on an industry or career, whether it be the world of modern art or computers to get the inside story of the people and the industry and how they react and interact. What is your character's dream? How does your character realize his or her dream?

How does the person achieve goals in the wake of the event, scandal, or other true story happening? Take your reader beyond the headlines and sound bits. Discover your character in your story and show how readers also can understand the person whose life story you're writing.

It makes no difference if it's your own or another's. You may want to bring out your story's texture more by adding a pet character and focusing also on the pet's reactions to your characters. For further information, below is a list of several book publishers and magazines in the field of religious and inspirational markets. Contact the various inspirational or religious booksellers associations, publishers associations, and religious or ethnic publishers associations.

Some Religious and Spiritual Book Publishers

Abingdon Press
Augsburg Fortress Publishing
Baker Book House
Behrman House
Bethany House Publishers
ChariotVictor Publishing
Dharma Publishing
Discipleship Resources
Feldheim Books
Gefen Publishing House Ltd.
Gospel Advocate Company
Hachai Publishing
Hazelden Publishing Group
Herald Press
Hope Publishing House
InterVarsity Press
Jason Aronson Inc. Publishers
Jewish Lights Publishing
Jewish Publication Society
Jonathan David Co., Inc. Publishers Joy Publishing
Judson Press
Kar-Ben Copies
Ktav Publishing House
Liguori Publications
The Littman Library of Jewish Civilization
Llewellyn Publications
Moody Press
Numata Center
Paraclete Press
Paulist Press

Pilgrim Press
Pitspopany Press
Red Heifer Press
St. Anthony Messenger Press
Targum Press
Thomas Nelson
Tyndale House Publishers
United Methodist Publishing House
Urim Publications
Vendanta Press
Westminster John Knox
Zondervan Publishing House

Magazines

Alive Now

Angels on Earth

Bible Advocate

Campus Life Magazine

Catholic Digest

Celebrations

Christian Families Online

Christian Home & School

Christian Science Monitor

ChristianWeek

Catholic Peace Voice,

Catholic Rural Life,

Children's Ministry

Church Herald and Holiness Banner,

Companion Magazine

Expression Christian Newspaper

Green Cross Magazine

Guideposts for Kids

Indian Life,

Moody Magazine.

New Writing Magazine

Our Little Friend (Weekly take-home paper for 1-6 yr olds).

Presbyterian Record

Spiritual Life

Teens Mission Launch Pad

The Upper Room

The Quiet Hour Echoes

Related Links on the World Wide Web

Periodical Publishers
http://www.colc.com/pubbook/periodical.htm

Association of Jewish Book Publishers
http://www.avotaynu.com/ajbp.html

Christian Book Publishers
http://www.colc.com/Publish.htm

Secular Newspapers with Religion Editors
http://www.colc.com/pubbook/reli-ed.htm

26

Health

If you don't have insurance or need to save money on your health, make sure you take advantage of free health screenings offered at health fairs. Senior centers, shopping malls, health departments, and other health agencies or businesses have frequent health fairs. Some items you can get for free include blood pressure and bone density screenings, cholesterol and blood glucose readings, weight, and other measures.

Flu shots usually are given free or at very low cost to certain age groups such as older adults. Call each health fair and ask the requirements.

Many screenings don't have age requirements. Ask that copies of the reports be sent to you as well as your doctor. Keep a record of your numbers and measurements. Different health fairs emphasize screening for different health issues such as bone density, blood sugar, blood pressure, or other research. Your health department and the sponsors of the health fair will have the schedules.

Study the health Web sites for factual material that you can research in magazines and journals. Health food stores have free booklets and pamphlets on various supplements and health food products.

Use your public library to read about what foods and nutrients work best. Make use of any offers for paid-for DNA testing for ancestry. Some genealogy surname groups on the Web offer to pay for DNA tests for ancestry.

Find out whether your surname fits the projects being researched. These tests usually are for males, and the Y chromosome is tested for ancestry research connected to some surname groups. Ask the various DNA testing companies that emphasize testing for ancestry whether there is a surname group offering to pay for DNA Y chromosome ancestry tests for males with the same surname, if there's a project researching the ancestry of that particular surname.

27

Pamphlet & Booklet Publishing

Write and publish 72-page or 98-page pamphlets and booklets on contemporary issues, historic romances, pet training, animal behavior, parenting, or school-related subjects such as biographies of historical characters, ethnic studies, or any other subject of interest to a wide or niche audience.

Pamphlets can be of the general consumer type found at supermarket checkout counters or specialty pamphlets on how-to subjects. Or they can be genre fiction such as children's stories, romances, or biography. Another form of pamphlet is the one-act 45 minute play suitable for high-school drama classes.

Here's how to write and sell a fast-selling paperback 98-page (when published) pamphlet or booklet, the kind you see on supermarket impulse racks at the check stand. They can sell quite a number of copies, or you can sell them by mail order or online from your Web site.

Start by writing about twice the number of pages that will be published. For a 98-page booklet, about 196 double spaced typed pages produces, usually a single-spaced booklet with double spaces and headlines between the sections. You may come out with having to write less than 196 pages, it depends upon the font and size of the booklet. However, here are the dimensions you'll need.

The size of the booklet may either be six inches wide by nine inches in length or five and a half inches wide by 8 inches or 8 1/2 inches in length. Take your choice. The difference is that trade paperbacks of 6 by 9 inches fit on supermarket impulse racks at checkout counters, whereas the mass market paperbacks you see in supermarkets and book stores in the back areas on special 5 by 8 book-size racks are standard for novels in the mass paperback market.

Let's say you choose the 6 by 9 size, which is the best fit for the impulse check out stand supermarket size. It will also fit into gift shops and specialty store racks. You'll have a soft, glossy cover with your price, usually $2.99 printed on the upper right hand corner of the book cover. The title will be placed in the middle of the book cover toward the upper half. It will be centered and have a two-word to five-word title that speaks volumes about what's in your little paper book.

In the middle of the cover, explain in one short sentence in smaller font, about 24 point what your book shows people how to do. It must be a how-to book such as how to find and keep a soul-mate, or some other how-to theme.

Below the explanation is the author's name: by, Joe John or whatever name you want on the cover. Inside the cover on the left hand side you print the name of your publishing company. Assuming you're publishing the booklet yourself, put an intelligent-sounding two-word name for your publishing company such as Behavioral Digests and trade mark your publishing firm, even if it's only you at home.

Then under than you can put a longer publishing company name, just in case you want to publish other items besides these little paperback booklets. Put something light Published by International Palm-sized Books, Inc., and your address. You can incorporate your publishing company. Use an office address or a PO Box number, not your home address. You don't want people showing up on the front steps.

Under that write: "Copyright, the year, by, your publishing company, address and e-mail address." Leave out your home phone. You can add a disclaimer in small font at the bottom that "Reproduction in whole or part of any (your publishing company's name) without written authorization is prohibited. Then add at the bottom, "printed in the USA" or wherever you send the booklet to be printed. I understand printing prices in Singapore are great, so I hear from greeting card publishers nowadays.

On your first page's right hand side, print the name of the book centered up close to the top of the page, leaving a 2 inch margin from the top. Put in a small clip art illustration or your own art, and then a line and a by (author's name) at the bottom, leaving another 2 inch margin from the bottom.

The left hand side of the first page can have an illustration centered. On the right hand side put your table of contents. Label it Contents. Divide your booklet into six small chapters and list them. Let's say your book is on how to find a rich mate. Label it with a title, such as why am I single? Then have a second chapter on your cure-all for loneliness.

A third chapter on raising your feeling of importance, a fourth chapter on how to appreciate being by yourself in various settings, a fifth chapter on how to find your soul mate and where to look, and a last or sixth chapter on how to keep your mate once you found him or her. Mostly women will buy this book on impulse, but if the book is labeled, how to pick up girls, of course it will attract guys or anyone who wants to meet girls.

The left hand side of your table of contents page should have artwork on it centered. Then on page 7, a right-hand side page, your first chapter begins with the title, self-explanatory and short, usually asking a question which you will answer in your first chapter. Define your question and answer it. Keep each chapter four printed pages, which is eight double spaced type written pages. When made single-spaced, each chapter runs to about four printed pages each.

Then start your second chapter on page eleven. Break your booklet up into segments or chunks. The printing will be singled spaced with double spaces between each section or segment heading that tells the reader how to solve a problem or fill a need. The problem could be technical or personal, business-oriented or relationship-oriented, health-directed, or about healing and nutrition, parenting, or any subject likely to land on a supermarket check out counter's impulse rack.

After every 14 or 14 chapters, usually 13 to 15 chapters, you'll need a segment or section break with a new title, perhaps outline your case histories, success stories, anecdotes, interviews, or using someone as an example. Don't use real names unless you have signed permission letters and can footnote that at the end of each chapter in a list of references that's numbered. For brevity, use a first name only and an initial, usually a fake false name approved by whomever you interview with an asterisk saying the name was changed to preserve privacy.

Use more than one example, usually two or three case histories. You can also use celebrity examples if you can get permission for success stories that run about 13 paragraphs each.

Have sections divided if you can around page 19, 21, 23, and start another chapter heading around page 28. Every two pages should have section breaks with new headings. You might write and publish a booklet on journaling and describe how it's related to a feeling of self-importance or of accepting oneself as "good," or write a technical or business how-to if you're not an expert on relationships.

More women will buy these booklets if they're about relationships. You can focus on instructional booklets on any topic from needlepoint and crafts to how to paint furniture and offer it to do-it-yourself stores, such as the big chain stores that customers frequent to buy do-it yourself materials for home repair and building. Another fast-selling area is travel writing.

This would focus on where to go and how to find specifics from antiques to restaurants and entertainment for various ages, education, visual anthropology, or special needs, such as traveling with multiple disabilities or traveling with one's dog or cat. One person trains his cat to use any toilet so he can take it into motel rooms without a litter box.

Your main focus is on how to do something, build something, solve a problem, make choices, or fill various needs, from quilting to relationships. Most people buy booklets with general titles such as how to keep a mate from leaving or how to save a troubled marriage.

Your six-chapter booklet should take up about 98 pages when printed, so don't make it longer or it won't fit into the small books rack in supermarkets and gift shops. It's easier to mail that way. Break your six chapters into three sections that run about two pages each per section with each chapter about four to six pages in length, but vary the length throughout the booklet.

Distribute it yourself or find a distributor who handles the supermarket impulse checkout counter rack. Or you can use gift shops or mail order. Another way to go is to offer your booklet to the tabloids as they have publishing divisions for these type of little books. They'll take a lot of your profit, so my advice is do everything yourself from writing to selling.

A print run of 1,500 copies would test your markets, but do your market research first to make sure someone would buy your book in large numbers. You might try a test run in a supermarket to see if the booklet moves and whether it competes with the tabloid-published booklets of similar size and length.

Will the tabloids let you compete with them in their supermarket client's racks? If not, you have the small gift shops and the malls. If you want to move the booklet, also offer it on tape or online for the e-publishing download market or on a CD ROM or DVD disk. Look at all the marketing alternatives and give your booklet visibility in place where people gather. Career booklets belong in community college and high school career counseling libraries.

Non-Fiction Booklets and Pamphlet on Controversial or Contemporary Issues

Write and publish sixty-six-page pamphlets or booklets that are about 4 inches wide and about 6 inches in length. These booklets fill up quickly with your articles. Don't forget to reduce the number of pages you write that first start out as double-spaced typed pages.

You can also provide marketing research for corporations or information for advertising and public relations agencies, employment agencies, or college career centers in this format or mystery shopper news if updates aren't required more frequently than annually.

If you're printing up an 8 1/2 by 11 inch page, usually it takes up to twice as much writing to reduce the size in half when you print up single spaced content with a double space between paragraphs and allow for a 16 point type size font for each heading or larger fonts for chapter headings.

Make Small Booklets with Fresh Information

When you print up small booklets, you'll need much less writing to fill up a whole little booklet. These small booklets are bought by school libraries to fill research folders on a variety of topics that are current issues in the news. If you are marketing to the general public through supermarket racks on impulse shelves near the checkout counter, usually near the checkout person, you'll want to supply each supermarket with your own racks the size of your tiny booklets.

The subjects that sell best are topics that tell the reader how something affects or changes something else. For example, how different foods affect your moods, and subtitle the booklet how people can change their behavior or their lives by adjusting the foods to their moods or any other topic telling readers how to improve themselves with the specific information.

Price your booklets anywhere from $1 to $2. Usually $1.19 in the US and $1.49 in Canada is fine, keeping the price plus tax adding up to an even amount. Find out what the tax would be on your booklets to one person at a checkout counter for the booklet. Then adjust the price so the reader can pay the tax and your price and have it add up to an easy to come up with amount, like $1.20 or $1.50. Calculate your expenses so you can arrive at a price that looks inviting.

Keep your pages around 66. Use an even number of pages. Your cover would have a title and a subtitle explaining what the title can do for the reader, how changing the behavior can change the person's life. Print your company or publishing name and address on the inside cover in the center.

On the first page, label it "Contents" and list you six or seven chapters and the page numbers. At the bottom of the contents page, about two inches up from the bottom of the page have the authors name in small, but easily readable font, such as 10 point Times New Roman or italics.

The left hand side of the contents page should have a disclaimer saying that your book is intended as a reference volume, not a medical manual so you won't be sued for giving medical advice without a license or credentials. Put in there that your booklet doesn't presume to give medical advice.

You really need this in there. Add a "consult your physician before beginning any therapeutic program," to protect yourself from being sued or accused of giving medical advice. You need this disclaimer on any booklet that gives information based on material provided by actual researchers and experts, even if you are using medical articles with simplified English or anything where people are told what to eat to change their health or behavior.

Always put this disclaimer or a similar one into a booklet you write and publish. This is especially true when you interview doctors or read their articles and report what they wrote, even with their written permission, which you always need to have. You don't need this disclaimer of your booklet is about how to knit costumes for animals or how to fix a leaky faucet or repair and antique furniture, but you need it for special diet, food, and nutrition booklets.

Each chapter can run four to 12 pages in this tiny booklet with the chapter divided every few paragraphs into new headings so you break up your booklet in chunks. Try to balance the size of your chapters. Usually four-page chapters work best in this size booklet totaling about 6 or 7 chapters, and total amount of pages being about 66.

Keep your pages an even number. Don't leave blank pages in this size booklet. Place a one or two-sentence description of the booklet centered about one inch down from the top of your glossy back cover.

Put it in a box if you like, and place or print your bar code below with the price on the back. You'll also have the price on the front cover, your logo in the upper left hand corner of the front cover, the title, subtitle, and any illustration, usually a photo in color of a person working with the items in the book or doing some action that sums up what the book says.

Have the book cover put on with two staples in the spine that are not readily noticeable to the reader. Only the backs of the staples should be seen on the spine, and flat into the crease of the spine of the book so as not to catch on any object. You don't need an ISBN number for this kind of booklet, only a bar code so the scanning machine in the supermarket can scan it. Provide your own racks if ones there belong to other merchants and distributors. Have the price on the front and back cover in addition to the bar code so readers can see the price immediately.

If you write on health topics, keep the English simple, writing at 5th grade level. Keep sentences short and paragraphs short, about two sentences per paragraph. Use Times New Roman 12 point type, nothing smaller, or older people won't want to look unless they have their reading glasses. So keep the font large enough for most people to see at most ages.

You can find distributors who specialize in small pamphlets and booklets. Print your own catalogue listing all your pamphlet/booklet titles. Place a catalogue copy on the Internet's Web to reach people around the world. Specialize in supplying college and high school career counseling offices with booklets on each type of career in a group of related careers. Or focus on foods and health or psychology and behavior for self-help.

Inspirational, religious, New Age, nutritional, and holistic health booklets each have individual, customized, expanding markets associated with conferences, conventions, suppliers, vendors, publications, and members of the various groups with similar interests.

If you want people to pay for your booklets, give readers information that's not easy to find and is not usually found among the free literature available in health food stores, community centers, self-help magazines, or religious organizations. Also try specialty gift stores, home building centers, discount stores, libraries, business, professional, and trade associations, corporations, schools, and employee organizations.

Supermarkets have special display racks with informational booklets and short romances. Some of these publishers are parts of larger publishing companies, such as the tabloids. Try gift shops, museums, libraries, bookstores, schools, churches, hotel lobby shops, sports stores such as golf and tennis shops at hotels and resorts, golf courses, and sports clubs.

Keep trying the supermarkets and smaller convenience stores until you find a store that lets you put in your own display rack for your catalogue of booklets or pamphlets. Sometimes used bookstores will allow you to put in a display case or rack of your short romances or historical fiction. School supply stores may be interested in your pamphlets with biographies of historical characters or vocational biographies.

Writing on contemporary and controversial issues in the news supplies school libraries with information for student research. Pamphlets need a bar code and a price more than they need an ISBN, but you can get one in case you want your booklet to go to libraries and schools or be sold by online booksellers and distributed by national distributors.

Sweet Romance Stories as Booklets

Keep trying to set up a display rack near check-out counters of stores. These are called the impulse racks. Turn your sweet or historical romance stories into a 4 inch by 6 inch small, 72-page booklets of either collected stories or one novelette, and sell your work in supermarkets and gift shops, candy gift stores, or packaged with other products. Don't forget those wonderful romance novelettes and stories you have that are shorter than book length.

Promote them on holidays such as St. Valentine's Day. Take your booklets to romance writers' conventions and club meetings. Write and publish pamphlets of holiday stories for Christmas, Easter, or any other religious holiday with appropriate stories or historical research articles. Promote them a month before the holidays. Animal stories are good such as cat or dog stories for Christmas or other holiday themes.

If they are sweet romances, short stories in three parts or "acts," of about 23 pages for each act, totaling around 72 pages or so, you can turn them into 72-page, 4 inch by 6 inch booklets, promote, and sell the little pamphlets at supermarkets. They go in the impulse racks at the checkout counters. Most of these small size mini-racks hold booklets about four inches wide by six inches long. This is the ideal size for romance stories or novelettes.

You'll get about a maximum of 300 words on a page: that's a maximum of 10 or 11 words across a line and about a maximum of 30 lines on a page. For first pages of new sections, and you'll have three sections or "acts," you start about two inches down from the top of the page with the first letter of your beginning sentence capitalized and highlighted in a larger font than the rest of the letters.

Print or place a bar code on the back of each booklet. It's a good idea to get an ISBN. It's a number placed on the back cover of books used as a code to find the book or to locate it in The Library of Congress and in the catalogue of the original publisher. Publishers, libraries, and book sellers locate books through that number. You don't necessarily need an ISBN unless you want to send your booklets to gift shops, libraries, schools, booksellers, or other publishers.

You'll need or put your own racks up to match your customized size in supermarkets if they have room, but the small size that holds the four by six inch booklet is fine.

How to Get an IBSN for Your Book, Pamphlet, or Booklet

If you plan to sell your booklet by mail order to gift shops in hospitals or to libraries, get the ISBN as well as the bar code. The ISBN is a unique machine-readable identification number, which marks any book.

If you need instructions on how to send away for an ISBN number to print on the back cover of your booklet, contact the national or regional ISBN agency in your own country. Presently, more than 160 countries or territories are official ISBN members. Check out the Web site of ISBN information titled, How to Get an IBSN number at: http://www.isbn-international.org/en/howtoget.html. The site for the USA regional office is at: http://www.isbn-international.org/en/agencies/usa.html. It's called The ISBN Agency for the United States. And it's in operation since 1968. It is located at the R. R. Bowker Co., LLC. Write to them at the following address:

R.R. Bowker Co., LLC
Att. Ms. Doreen Gravesande
Senior Director ISBN/SAN/PAD
630 Central Ave.
New Providence, NJ 07974
Tel: Toll Free/United States: 877-310-7333
    All others: (+1 908) 286-1090
Fax: (+1 908) 219-0188
E-mail: isbn-san@bowker.com
URL: http://www.isbn.org

Decide whether you'd like to put an ISBN on the back cover of your book or only a bar code and the price. A typical booklet that is four inches wide by six inches in length has no ISBN number on the back cover. Instead, it has the price and a bar code at the bottom. In the middle of the back cover would be a title and subtitle and three sentences or two paragraphs explaining the main message of your booklet or pamphlet. The typical number of pages would be about 66 for this type of booklet.

The size is suitable for supermarket racks. One excellent example is a booklet titled *What Do Dogs Dream About?* It is published by Mini Mags in Boca Raton, Florida, copyrighted in 2000. The back cover tells you what the booklet is about. And it has a bar code and price on the back cover. The last page contains a box with the sentence: "We Want Your Cute Dog Stories."

When you publish your booklet, use the bottom of the last page, if space allows, to ask readers for feedback and to collect ideas and stories for your next pamphlet. And always obtain written permission from anyone who sends you anything before you use it in any way. A good way to collect ideas or stories is to run writing contests and publish the winning story. Decide what the prize will be and whether one-time publishing rights would be what the author and you agree on. Or work only with your own stories.

Writing and Publishing Your Own Sweet or Historical Romances or Biographies

Here's how to organize your little book of sweet romances or biographies of historical characters. The cover should be a glossy heavier weight paper that can fold easily enough to fit into a small pocket or purse so people can carry the book easily onto transportation.

Market your book at racks in airports, train, and bus stations or at transit centers in vending machines if you buy the empty ones and place them where you can get permission. Hotel lobbies have racks that could fit your book, but usually you supply your own racks to hotels and convention centers.

Resorts and antique malls also are great places for your little book. Tourist attraction shops in the "old town" sections of cities are great. In fact any place that sells tourist souvenirs make great places to sell your little romances. People staying in hotels and motels can read the little books, and you can offer the same size booklets with adventure stories or romances related to the particular town or resort history.

On the cover have an illustration in color of the couple featured in the romance story, usually a cameo of the couple featured against a pristine background of countryside, or local resort attractions. On the top you can put a ribbon-like title "Your (logo or name) Romance Library" or "Historical Romances of the resort city___" or whatever you want to feature as your own publishing and writing library.

This represents your collection of booklets. You can publish your own writing or those from other romance or historical fiction writers. Travel booklets, auto travel games for kids, or travel romances also can be published in this format.

Usually sweet romances sell better than other genres in this type and size of booklet. People want a sweet romance to escape to and to read at night, especially people traveling on business at hotels. The books will be bought by women and female students of all ages, with the highest demographic being in the 18 to 44 age range and the next highest, 44 to 54 age range.

To help sell your romance against the competition, put in a pet character, usually a cat or kitten or a pair of cats in the story that bring the couple together. Your story can feature a female who works at an animal shelter. In this way you can bring in a real animal shelter and dedicate your booklet to animal rescue volunteers, which helps move the story. You can also donate a percentage of your income from the booklet to help animal rescue shelters of your choice.

Make sure your story is universal and familiar enough to sell anywhere in the country or even overseas. Your booklet also can be translated into languages if you sell to various countries. Keep your pamphlet-sized library focused on sweet romance. These supermarket rack pamphlets appeal to a wider and older audience than the actual full-length romance novels found in bookstores.

People want to believe that love, commitment, and faith in your ability to hold a family together while standing on your own two feet and pulling your weight conquers all. People buy these little stories to relax, to be nourished, to feel good and important and to escape the real world. Yet the story must be real enough so that it could believably happen to the reader.

Your little booklet will be a tiny version of a magazine. In the romance story, keep it around 72 pages as the best-size and weight for handling, mailing, and reading in one sitting. Most people will buy these as they leave the supermarket to take with them during that long hour or two wait in doctors and dentists offices or while taking a two-hour train ride or while on vacation on the beach or in a hotel or during anytime when waiting is necessary.

The non-fiction informational booklet can be around 66 pages in length. It's not going to make a difference whether your pages run to 66 or 72 as long as the last page isn't a blank waste of space and the two staples on the spine that binds the glossy front and back covers will easily hold together the booklet.

How to Format Your Book or Booklet Manuscript

Start your story halfway down page 3 with the title of your little book. You'll find about six paragraphs can fit on one page. In a sweet romance story, don't have chapter headings or a table of contents. Instead of chapter headings, you only have the title page with author's name and dedication "to the____." Fill in to whomever you dedicate the story.

Use three asterisks (***) at the end of each part or chapter of the story instead of chapter headings. The asterisks represent the breaks in the story when the action changes instead of having chapter headings. Your story can run about an average of 23 to 26 pages before the chapter ends with the three asterisks and new action begins, for example, on page 27. Then run the action on to about page 36 and have three asterisks there.

On page 38 the first sentence starts about two inches down with the first letter of the first sentence in larger and highlighted capital letters than the rest of the text. Your middle chapter ends about on page 62 with page 63 started with new action about two inches in margin from the top of the page and the first letter of the first sentence in highlighted, larger capital letters.

You'll notice that the book or story has three acts or three parts. Each chapter can be of unequal or equal length. It doesn't matter as long as it adds up to a total of about 72 pages. So you see, the sweet romance story has, like a full-length stage play or short cinema film, 72 pages made up of three acts. Each act takes up a third of the booklet or story. You have a beginning, middle, and end. It follows the rules for a romance novel with romantic push- and- pull tension between the characters.

In the story you bring together an unlikely couple that conquer the push and pull tension of first impressions that don't prove true as you flesh out the second and third act where sweet romance proves love conquers all.

Build up your own romance library of titles from your own writing or those of other authors. Some authors might want to start a cooperative where they share the cost of publication and distribution, but this is up to you.

You'd do well with only your own stories and publishing your own work. Distribute to supermarkets and gift stores. Then add other sources such as racks in hotels, waiting rooms, airports, hospitals, senior centers, community centers, bus or train stations, cruise ships' libraries, schools, or doctors' and dentists' offices, lawyers' offices, and any place people travel or wait, including tourist gift stores in resort areas and theme parks.

Book stores and libraries or vending machines in rest rooms or on the street near supermarkets are good bets for little books. Romance novelettes should run around 72 pages. Keep them even numbers. On the back cover place a two paragraph review of each character the starring male and female of the couple and tell something about the person in one sentence for each character. Use only two characters on the back cover.

Your third paragraph, a one-sentence statement tells what the story is about in a 15-word sentence that is centered in the middle of the page. Below this three sentence/three paragraph description, put a short statement about your romance library or book, such as "welcome to a cornucopia of sweet romance, where love brings different people together" or love conquers all (this one has been used on Mini-Mags).

So use your own original statement, "romance unites all." Pick your own logo. The bar code goes at the bottom of your back cover, usually in the lower left hand corner. Your own logo image goes at the lower right hand corner. Put your banner and initials centered beneath your "Welcome to the world of sweet romance" or other statement. Use your own statement, not the one Mini-Mags uses. Use them for inspiration only or marketing research.

On your front cover have your banner and logo, an illustration in the center, and your price at the lower left hand corner. Pick your own prices, but don't go over $2.00 or you won't compete with the $1.59 of the current ones. Have your 72-page romance novelettes or stories bound.

Don't use staples in a fiction booklet. That's only for how to booklets or tiny pamphlets on how to change something or improve one's behavior or booklets on food and nutrition or health. So be sure to have a bound booklet for romance that has no staples. Research the booklets in existence and show your printer.

This is one way to find winning strategies or guerilla tactics to salvage your wonderful stories if they are rejected and you know they are really as good or better than similar stories in print and selling wonderfully.

If you have revised your stories and have logical reasons and concrete research and marketing tests showing the content appeals to all audiences and could sell well if published, then a 72-page romance story printed and promoted would cost you far less than publishing a romance novel with no way to distribute it.

Do your research first. Talk to distributors, and find out how to get your small racks into supermarkets or other sources where you can sell them. Try news stands and vending machines or packaging your romance stories. Other products can be packaged with your booklet and offered as promotions. These might include honeymoon packages, lingerie, and mail order products such as gift baskets for bridal showers or booklets sold at writer's conventions.

You can review audio books and send the 110-word reviews to magazines publishing audio book reviews. Concentrate on the audio presentation and narrator rather than on the literary print format for an audio book review. Pamphlets and booklets can be converted to audio format.

You can narrate your own stories or informational pamphlets on audio CDs and market them alone or as package deals with other products or books. Audio material should run an hour on each CD, MP3 CD, DVD, or other format. Most people need a break after listening for an hour. Some tapes and CDs run about an hour and a half. Keep yours in that parameter, an hour to an hour and a half of listening, similar to a feature film.

Formatting Book Manuscripts for an Editor

Here's how to format a book manuscript. The acquisitions editor will hand your book to a group of readers after spending about 20 seconds getting a first impression. Your book manuscript is read as if it were a resume. They expect white 20 pound 8.5" X 11x" paper without textures. The acquisitions editor will photocopy your outline, proposal, synopsis, cover letter, and sample chapters or if fiction, completed book when requested.

If the paper weighs more than 20 pounds, it will be hard to photocopy, and thin, onion-skin paper will tear in the automatic photocopying machine. If you're in another country, send a clear photocopy of your work on this type of paper, if possible. Your book, again, is your resume and application for a business partnership or employment and needs to reflect that business mood.

The cover page will contain your book title, the division of the publishing house for which your book is intended, and the number of words and pages. You put your name and address on the cover sheet and the date. After your cover page, insert a blank sheet and put another blank sheet after the last page to protect the last page of your book from creasing and tearing.

My favorite romance of this size is author, Kathleen Dreesen's sweet romance story, *Loving Touch*. It runs the standard 72 pages, and the novelette booklet is published by American Media Mini Mags Inc., MicroMags logo. Her booklet is dedicated to the staff and volunteers at We Care Animal Rescue, St. Helena, California. The characters are fiction. Only their love is real, says the statement on the first page. I highly recommend reading this booklet to get an idea of the size and type of story that sells well.

On the inside of your cover, put your name, business address, and email. Put the date of the copyright and where it was printed, in the USA or elsewhere. Your title page would have the title centered, the author's name beneath it, and any dedication. On the back of your title page, print any information regarding your decision to accept or not accept unsolicited manuscripts from other writers.

Otherwise, you may get everyone sending you their romance stories in hopes you'll publish them. You don't want your mail or email blocked, so print a statement that you'll only take one-page queries if you're interested, or whether you don't want anyone sending you their own stories to publish.

Editors want a standard of one inch margins all around each page, on everything. Leave room for the reader's and editor's notes on top of the page. Your header is standardized at one inch from the top page and a half inch higher than where your text starts. Make sure your header is the same width as the text line.

On this page, you put the title of your book, your name, and the page number on the upper right corner. Use your full or last name (last name is preferred by most editors). Use the same font throughout, preferably Times New Roman 12 point.

Don't send books in any other font as editors are required to convert for typesetting departments to Times New Roman 12. So convert it if it's in Courier, Ariel or another font. Make sure the font is as black as you can get it and the paper is really white, not tan. It has to be photocopied without a shadow.

Most books accepted had more white space and paragraphs under ten lines. Rejected books almost always didn't have these appearances. When mailing your book, put it in a clear plastic bag, the kind you get from the supermarket or meat counter, with no printing on the bag.

The green or red printing comes off with moisture and ruins the book with stains. So no print is placed on the bag. After your book is in the clear plastic (transparent) bag, fold it over so it fits well around the book and put a small bit of transparent tape in the middle. Then put two rubber bands around your manuscript. One rubber band will be at the top and the other at the bottom to hold the plastic bag in place better and to keep pages together.

Don't send a manuscript in a loose leaf binder and don't put clips on it. Leave off any file folders. Put the manuscript along with a sturdy self-addressed stamped envelope inside a large envelope with book padding. Make sure the return envelope won't tear in shipping and handling when it's returned. Have the correct number of stamps on the envelope.

Also add to this before sealing, a self-addressed stamped post card the editor can return to let you know your book is received. You'd be surprised at the long way this courtesy goes and the effect it has on readers or editors about your attitude to save them the postage of a receipt reply. Print up some business cards and put this into a small envelope with your return card, so you'll look more like a professional writer with a business card.

Have a query letter or cover letter on top of everything so the editor will know what you want done with the book and what it's about, and perhaps a guide to the synopsis. In one paragraph or preferably one sentence, state or pitch what your book is about: For example, it has been said that "Star Trek is Wagon Train in Space."

Never embarrass an editor by sending a gift or artsy crafty item with a manuscript because everything will be returned after going in the slush pile. Manuscripts must never be faxed. They use up the editor's paper supply and make an awful impression on your attitude and boldness. You want to make an impact of courtesy and business-like manners, an aura of professionalism.

Every time someone faxes a manuscript or synopsis, usually it's rejected and taken as an insult for tying up the fax machine and using up the paper at the other end. So treat your manuscript as if it were your best resume. Show your enthusiasm by a professional, business-like attitude and common courtesy.

28

Playography

DESCRIPTION OF BUSINESS:

How would you like to work on cruise ships showing passengers and crew how to play for stress reduction and health benefits or work at home selling your play-for-health videos? Your videos can improve the quality of life for others. Wouldn't it be wonderful to make a video on the healing power of play (playography) linking research with dolphins and autistic children to show beneficial mutual effects? Your videos help therapists take clients to the next level of recovery.

The video therapist technician assists a psychologist, interpreter for the deaf, psychiatrist, social worker, counselor, teacher, or psychotherapist by operating a video camera, editing the tape, and monitoring a television set to help children and adults with emotional or behavioral problems. In some videos people and animals interact to show the beneficial or healing results from play between the two.

Scriptwriting is another option. The best market today is producing and distributing exercise, fitness, or healing-through-play videos for target populations and special groups of clients or patients such as preschool, seniors, persons with certain illnesses or disabilities.

Video therapy is done also with schizophrenics to show them how to have emotion, and with the elderly for therapeutic communication. It is a new biofeedback technique that teaches speech volume and coping mechanisms. It condenses behavior into "well" role models on video tape and shows a person how others see him or her.

Video therapy teaches pro-social behavior in prisons, schools, geriatric homes, on-the-job, in psychologists' offices, and in numerous institutional settings. Experience is telescoped. The video therapist's duties are to film the counseling session and carefully to edit the tape to include only appropriate behavior.

The patient then sees the edited tape and becomes his or her own teaching resource. It's also important to videotape interpreters for the deaf as they do their hand and finger signing in American Sign Language.

These interpreters need to be videotaped so that the speaker in the background of the tape can be hand signed for deaf video viewers. Or you can close-caption video tapes and put in written words on the tape.

INCOME POTENTIAL:

A video therapist technician can create applications and uses for niche markets in video therapy, virtual reality, and fitness. As a video therapist technician you can write and/or produce training materials and multimedia for home-based persons or for people who work with a wide variety of clients in the self-help field. Create your own videos and sell them each in the range of $20 to $40 to helping professionals, allied health workers, and the public.

BEST LOCALE TO OPERATE THE BUSINESS:

Institutional centers, childhood development centers, schools, geriatric centers, psychiatrist's offices, marketing and advertising research firms, cable television stations, exercise spas, and educational psychology research programs.

Exercise, acupressure, Yoga, and playography videos appeal to stressed-out salespersons, therapists, teachers, attorneys, public speakers, holistic health workers, nurses, physicians, and other allied health workers, sedentary people, and anyone interested in personal growth, fitness, or nutrition.

Operate your video business or distribute your tapes in areas where holistic health and alternative fitness instruction is popular—such as large cities, the whole state of California, the entire West coast, New York, large cities, ski resorts, health spas, vacation areas, Colorado, and especially, Arizona.

TRAINING REQUIRED:

Video school courses in camera operation and videotape editing are helpful. By learning how to edit videotape, you can save yourself the cost of hiring a video editor.

Many video production supplies stores offer short courses in how to edit tape and in video production techniques. They can also refer you to low-cost adult education courses in the community.

Community college courses in recreational therapy assisting, gerontology, or nursery school teaching also are helpful

You can even earn a certificate as a "certified" recreational therapy aide or recreational therapist from a community or two-year college and produce videos on recreation for the institutionalized person or for senior centers and nursing homes. In addition, you can earn a certificate as a health and fitness trainer or health promoter from the extended studies division of many major universities. Extension courses (extended studies departments) are open to adults and usually have no-prerequisites.

GENERAL APTITUDE OR EXPERIENCE:

The ability to relate to all kinds of people under extremes of behavior is essential. An aptitude for editing video in an artistic way following specific directions is necessary.

VIDEO EQUIPMENT NEEDED:

Purchase a broadcast quality video camera or super digital high 8 camcorder or DVD camcorder, video tape, editing machine, VCR player, computer for desktop video, and equipment to produce titles on your videotape. This can be either standalone title makers or computer software that produces titles on videotape and can be hooked up to your video camera. Call your local video supplies store to outfit you with camera, editing machines, title makers, and tape.

It's important that your video doesn't lose quality the more times it's played. Don't use a VHS home camcorder because the tapes lose quality when reproduced and when played over and over. You'll be making many copies of your tapes for distribution to a wide variety of helping professionals.

OPERATING YOUR BUSINESS:

How would you like to work on cruise ships showing passengers and crew how to play for stress reduction and health benefits? Contact psychotherapists, hypnotherapists, prison wardens, psychiatrists, hospitals, schools for special education, speech pathology centers, rehabilitation centers, psycho-dramatists and schools teaching psychodrama, art therapy, or the expressive and recreational therapies, home healthcare nursing departments of hospitals and home care agencies, nursing homes, senior citizens centers, recreational facilities, hospices, fitness centers, weight loss centers, nutrition companies, holistic health clinics, acupuncture schools, allied health care schools, and crises centers to find a therapist you can apprentice to as a video therapy technician.

You can teach Yoga exercises, acupressure, infant massage, exercises for pregnant women or senior citizens, holistic health, personal growth, preschooler's fitness training, alternative fitness techniques, playography (geographic diversity of types of play and their applications) or playology (the healing power of play) for beginners, seniors, the disabled, children, or any targeted audience.

Put the Yoga or acupressure instruction or other mild, stretching exercises on tape for relaxation or rehabilitation. Asian exercises such as Yoga or Tai Chi Chuan (Chinese slow exercises favored by seniors) are available on tape. Read studies of how Tai Chi for mature adults helps strengthen their ability to balance.

There are health benefits to certain other exercises that you could interview people about to make an instructional video. The type of exercise varies from belly dancing to Yoga and Tai Chi to wheelchair aerobics.

You can become an independent practitioner of exercise technology. Call the local spas, nursing homes, assisted living centers, and gerontology-oriented social and community centers. Ask whether they can hire you to work as a video therapist exercise technician. Or make a video on a DVD and offer the video to these types of establishments. Work with the elderly in homes, spas, and gerontology centers.

A decade later, we find acupressure, playography, Yoga, Tai Chi Chuan (Chinese exercise), infant massage, preschool children's exercise, exercises for pregnant women, and slow Oriental exercises for senior citizens tapes popular and in demand by people seeking alternative ways to physical fitness, personal growth, and relaxation techniques.

For example, infant massage tapes and exercise videos for pregnant women can be sold in maternity clothes stores. Alternative exercise tapes for senior citizens can be sold in stores and community centers older people frequent, and playography videos can be marketed at hospital workshops where patients learn stress release techniques or in classes, that nurses, psychologists, and social workers attend to fulfill continuing education licensing renewal requirements.

Playology videos focus on discovering the healing power of laughter and play, especially for people suffering from the fear of play. Playography videos emphasize the diverse and similar types of play around the world, at different periods of history, or within various ethnic groups. You could make videos using scientific data validating the healing power of play, including problem solving by using the creative process.

Compare play among tribal peoples or in contrasting areas of the world such as India, Scandinavia, Africa, Latin America, the USA, Australia, Oceania, the Middle East, Central Asia and Europe. Your videos could help viewers lighten up and learn to play more, laugh to promote health, and have fun wherever they happen to be at the moment in order to relieve stress.

Ellie Katz, R.N., PhD coined the word "*playology.*" Highly recommended is her wonderful 10-minute video, "*Change Your Mind,*" on the healing power of laughter and play. Ellie Katz traveled all over the world giving *playology* workshops and seminars on cruise ships.

Her 10-minute video is on the subject of how to play in your office, home, with groups, and how to stay healthy, do what you are and get better. The field of *playology,* (the healing power of play and laughter) or *playography* (defined as the geographic and demographic study of play) are field open for you to make videos, audios or other learning materials, including board games.

Show others how to get over the fear of playing and how to use scientific data validating the healing power of play. Or show others in a video DVD how play is enjoyed in different areas of the world—a visual geography or anthropology of play.

In addition to play therapy, you can view the healing power of oriental exercise on video. If you don't know anything about Yoga or Tai Chi, then join a class at your community center or extended studies for life-long learning group. Rent a video on any of these relaxation and healing-oriented exercises. Study scientific and behavioral studies of play as a combination of relaxation, laughter, and mild exercise.

Work with an instructor to make a video of any new approaches to healing or stress reduction through play or slow exercises. Make a video with the instructor giving beginning instructions on a 30 to 60 minute DVD, or produce a series of instructional video discs for beginners, intermediate, and advanced students.

Find out from the instructor, based on market surveys and the instructor's class numbers which tapes are most likely to sell—usually the beginner's tapes or intermediate. Variety for beginners is more important in the workouts than advanced studies that would appeal to fewer students.

Offer your services to work with the patients or clients in offering fitness or health-related videos for instructional or recreational purposes in the field of health and fitness, recreation, activities training, or creative and expressive arts.

When you find the centers you want to work for or the therapists you want to apprentice with, ask them what their specific needs are in video or videotaping to teach their clients pro-social behavior, such as self-esteem realities. Then produce the tapes to meet their exact requirements to help individual clients or patients. Video therapy is about transformation.

TARGET MARKET:

Find manufacturers of exercise equipment and ask them to include your videos prepackaged with their equipment. You can work out a barter deal with them so you can include your advertising on the back of your video package along with their advertising copy. Also ask specialty shops such as maternity or children's stores for permission to put your video display rack in their window or at their checkout counter for impulse buys as people pay for their merchandise.

Cooking videos frequently are sold along with new convection ovens. Exercise videos and booklets, or videos go well with prepackaged products.

Examples include the following:

Tai Chi Chuan
Infant massage
Pet massage,
Play for various age groups
Special interest organizations,
Exercise for pregnant women
Walking tours for older adults.

You can prepackage your video or instructional material with products related to exercise or relaxation equipment and healing music, memory-enhancing devices, furniture, sandals, clothing, appliances, and related types of devices and musical instruments. Some producers put relaxing sounds and sights, like nature and clouds with music on videotape for stress reduction.

Approach the maternity hospitals, birthing centers, or nurseries. Offer your video to new mothers leaving the hospital with their babies. Capture a niche market by focusing your tape on a subject like infant exercise and massage, exercises for postpartum women, acupressure, playography, tummy flattening tapes, or other health and fitness information on video appealing to a specifically targeted market interested in new possibilities for fitness.

Your videos can also come with booklets on the same subject or any type of exercise equipment, holistic health products, food supplements, etc. You could do demonstrations at holistic health fairs and conventions or rent booths to other videocassette producers at theme conventions.

Therapists, hospitals, prisons, and fitness centers use therapeutic video or interactive video to observe people interacting and to record their behavior for study, research, and therapy. You want to reach all helping professionals, such as the following:

1. interpreters for the deaf who want you to put their sign-language expert on videotape to explain their instructional tapes.

2. prison psychologists, who may want you to make a videotape about pro-social behavior and self worth training for the prison population.

3. speech pathologists who may want you to make videos to train stroke victims to look into mirrors to see their opposite hand and try to move it.

4. acupuncturists, acupressurists, and holistic health practitioners or alternative fitness experts who may ask you to make instructional videos for specific audiences.

5. cruise ships, airlines, hospitals, and nursing homes—who may wish to show your uplifting videos on how to improve the quality of life.

You can specialize in creating videos for children. Target preschools, children's centers, hospitals, and schools of education where preschool teachers are trained. Another specialty is creating exercise, fitness, and eating-the-right foods videos for preschoolers and children in daycare, nursery schools, after-school care, and at children's hospitals. Create a children's or preschooler's gym on video by targeting corporate daycare centers and gyms.

RELATED OPPORTUNITIES:

Recreational video exercise therapist, instructional media technologist, cable television programmer, playographer, cruise seminar and event planner, and holistic health practitioner videographer.

Your exercises could focus on preschoolers or infants. Appeal to family gym classes where parents take their infants for workouts and to learn more about play between parents and children. Provide videos so that the whole family, including grandparents can exercise together and get fit.

ADDITIONAL INFORMATION:

American Kinesiotherapy Association (exercise therapists)
259-08 148th Rd.
Rosedale, NY 11422
(718) 276-0721

American Association for Rehabilitative Therapy, Inc.
PO Box 6412
Gulf Port, Mississippi 39506

National Association of the Deaf
814 Thayer Ave.
Silver Spring, MD 20910
 (301) 587-1788

National Therapeutic Recreation Society
3101 Park Center Dr., Suite 1200
Alexandria, VA 22302
 (703) 820-4940

National Council for Therapeutic Recreation Certification
49 S. Main St., Suite 005
Spring Valley, NY 10977-5635
 (703) 914-3569

American Association of Advertising Agencies (AAAA)
666 Third Avenue, 13th floor
New York, NY 10017
(212) 682-2500

American Yoga Association
3130 Mayfield Rd., W-103
Cleveland Heights, OH 44118
1(800)226-5859 or (216) 371-0078

29

Pens

Instructions for making your own writing pen are on the Rockler.com Woodworking Superstore at: http://www.rockler.com/articles/display_article.cfm?&cookietest=1&&story_id=41.

You don't need a lathe to make your own custom pen. The instructions at the Web site come, with permission, from Alice's Workshop (Woodworking and Crafts) at: http://members.fortunecity.com/alices_workshop/. Basically, you cut in half a pen blank using your box and mitre saw. If you don't own a mitre saw, use what you have that will cut through a piece of material about a half inch in diameter. Pen blanks come in strips 5" X 1/2" X 1/2" wood or corian.

If you don't want to buy pre-cut pen blanks, then cut your own pen blank from 1/2" stock. Use scrap wood or corian. According to the Web site, you'll be "drilling a hole all the way through the center of both pieces lengthwise using a drill press and a 7 mm drill bit."

The site also mentions using a pen kit and also has a link to a *Jet Pen Lathe* that you can use to make your own pens and pencils. Pen turning can be a hobby or a business that makes customized pens. Make your own pens and pencils for your family, or make them to sell online or at swap meets. Also, you can make your own bleach pen by putting bleach in a fountain pen or dipping a dry, clean fine-pointed marking pen in bleach.

30

Permanent Plastic Seal

At the Web site ThriftyFun.com, there are thousands of tips, articles, and requests such as sealing plastic bags with foil and an iron. You just put the foil over the plastic bag parts that you want sealed and iron the spot with a warm iron. See the Web site for these handy tips at http://www.thriftyfun.com/tf644813.tip.html.

In the past I've always sealed my keepsakes to keep mice from eating cardboard or paper by placing any type of metal or aluminum foil over the plastic and sealing the plastic like a big laminating machine. It works well with garments sealed in plastic wrap as well. The kind of plastic bags that can be sealed don't come in all sizes in most supermarkets.

So you can make your own sealed plastic bags by ironing them. If you don't use aluminum foil or other metal over the plastic the warm iron will melt the plastic all over your fabric and probably rip fabric when you try to peel off the plastic. Always use something that will not melt when you put a warm iron on anything like plastic that can't take the heat without melting.

Once you seal the plastic by laminating, it's sealed until you rip it open. To make your own customized vinyl or plastic garment bags with zippers or Velcro, use an inexpensive roll of transparent plastic painter's drop cloth. Cut to the size you want and with fabric glue, glue in a zipper or Velcro.

Or sew in a zipper or Velcro using thread and sewing machine needles suitable for sewing on plastic or vinyl. If what you want to put in a garment-sized or customized bag is sensitive to ultra violet light from the sun or other lighting, use black or dark colored vinyl or plastic of the type used for table cloths. Buy from a fabric store to customize the size you want by buying the vinyl or plastic by the yard. Then blue or sew the zipper or Velcro at the top to seal in the garment, film, or whatever else you want to keep from light damage.

31

Pesticides—Home-Made from Spices and Vegetables

Cinnamon oil kills mosquitoes according to the Web site Dirt Doctor at http:// www.dirtdoctor.com/view_org_research.php?id=26. I first noticed how fast the mosquitoes disappeared when I bought air freshener spray made with cinnamon oil. See the article researching cinnamon oil as an insecticide in the July14, 2004 issue of the *Journal of Agricultural and Food Chemistry.* The study looked at essential oils such as cinnamon and catnip. Cinnamon oil is easier to find in household products.

It's amazing how popular Borax, boric acid, garlic, basil, and vinegar and cinnamon oil are as insect repellents. Citronella also wards off mosquitoes. Also see the Web site at: http://www.mercola.com/2004/aug/7/cinnamon_oil_deet.htm which compares cinnamon to Deet for mosquito control in your home.

An old recipe for getting rid of insects is to leave fresh basil leaves in the corners and behind furniture. Back on the farm, another recipe for getting rid of fleas in furniture and pet bedding recipe is to sprinkle Borax around a dog's blankets and bedding to get rid of fleas. Then vacuum it up so the dog doesn't lick the Borax.

Make your own non-toxic pesticides from natural ingredients. The Web site at eHow, http://www.ehow.com/how_4034_make-own-nontoxic.html gives recipes for using condiments and foods around the house to make non-toxic pesticide sprays. The pesticides last for a short time because they come from food products. So you can't store them. Spray them on, let dry, and reapply after the surface gets wet from rain or in the case of plants, from watering.

One of the recipes is to combine food ingredients such as chopped garlic and hot peppers or pepper sauce with a little liquid detergent and spray on a household surface to keep insects away. Another recipe for the garden is to blind three white onions and one garlic bulb with three cups of water. Then strain out the vegetables and use the water which should be left standing overnight. You can add enough water to make a gallon of liquid spray for your garden.

Other recipes for natural non-toxic (to humans) pesticides include mixing mineral oil with garlic cloves to make a spray on garden plants that are infested with bugs. It's the garlic that gets them to run, and the oil serves as a means of keeping the garlic essence working. Before you put anything on your garden plants test one to see how it reacts. Most plants are sensitive to soap and acid. So be cautious and wait before you put the solutions on all your plants.

The Web site at http://www.ehow.com/how_4033_rid-home-fleas.html shows you how to rid your house of fleas. Some of the recipes include boric acid. A simpler recipe is to mixing eight parts Borax cleaning powder with one part table salt. Sprinkle around and leave for a week before vacuuming several times. The salt and Borax mixture dries out the flea eggs and the area where the fleas live. Keep your pets and small children away from the areas that you sprinkle with the mixture.

You don't want people with respiratory problems breathing the Borax and salt in the air. And you don't want pets or children eating the Borax and salt mixture. Sprinkle the mixture on areas of the house you can vacuum, not on your pets' bodies.

See the Web site for the actual recipes. There are several there for making various types of pesticides that use ingredients made from vegetables and condiments or products you normally find around your home. Some handy tips at the Web site include preventing termites from invading your home by building sand barriers in crawl spaces and under fence posts, patios, and steps. According to the Web site, "Termites cannot tunnel through sand."

An abstract of a recent study published in Environmental Health Perspectives that's posted at the Care2 Web site at: http://www.care2.com/channels/solutions/guides/226, notes that 99 percent of children tested for that study show pesticide exposure. It's time to make natural pesticides from vegetables and spices.

Cinnamon and the skin of cucumbers are products also used to get rid of insects. Wood scraps draw termites, and cardboard and paper draw in mice. See the Coleoptera Web site at: http://www.coleoptera.org/p1020.htm. According to the Web site, "If ants are coming in through doors or windows, put a cinnamon stick across the path. They will not cross it." The site also has a tip noting that ceramic tile floors are too cold for mice and roaches to cross.

Other repellents mentioned on the Web site include garlic salt, a mix of borax and sugar on ant hills, and other combinations of food and detergents to get rid of bugs. Other tips include mixing bay leaves and Listerine mouthwash to get rid of cupboard ants. Wiping olive oil on plant leaves also helps repel bugs. Borax repels roaches and boric acid chases away ants. At the Antbuster.com Web site at: http://www.antbuster.com/ants-articles/ants-in-plants.asp, you'll find recipes for making ant-repelling with cinnamon. According to the site, "Cinnamon is both repugnant and fatal to ants."

32

Publicity & Promotion

How to you persuade the media to launch and pre-sell your creative work before you find a publisher, producer, agent, or manufacturer? To persuade the press, create an age-elated hub. This can be a mature adult, parenting, or teen hub. Look at any teen hubfrom the 1990s, such as Goosehead. There's still room for other shows like Goosehead, and one could feature your unpublished writing, learning, parenting, or merchandising ideas.

Create a similar venture yourself online by first developing the content. You could create content for shows similar to Goosehead or create your own concept. After call, a concept is actually made up of facts built around a foundation or basic message. Think of a concept as a sculpture built step-by-step over a wire frame skeleton.

The idea of a teen hub came about when a 14-year old girl named Ashley Power with her personal Web site caught the attention of Richard Dreyfuss. He made a deal to create content for Goosehead. How did such publicity come to a 14-year olds personal Web site?

Thousands of girls from 11 to 15 daily have personal Web sites and need content. One day actor Richard Dreyfuss's niece appeared in a Goosehead video series. It's quite a leap and rare that the niece of an actor appears in a video series that springs out of a 14-year old girl's Web site. Such rarity is what makes for fame. What part did destiny play? According to media reports, Dreyfuss got in touch with Power and made a deal to create at least two interactive episodes to Goosehead.

What can you do that's interactive? If you're a parent, start with what's familiar to you in parenting. Look at similar sites yourself, and decide what about it made the teen hub or senior citizen life-long learning hubs ripe. How did the concept of a teenage hub move from a 14-year old girl's personal Web site into a video series that caught the eye of a star who writes content for interactive Web?

The episodes, by the way, were called Webisodes. Actually, the technical term is multicasting content as opposed to multimedia that's not always online. Before you test the waters, look at the following sites that use stars to plug products they like. Then think of ways how you can *launch* your unpublished writing in the credible media by *plugging a product* you like and that a star also likes. Look at www.gooshead.com, www.babystyle.com, www.voxxy.com, www.sightsound. com, www.shockwave.com, and www.generationa.com. What did you notice about teen hub sites?

Is there anything similar you can do with your sites to produce content or plug a product you like for the age group you want to emphasize? Use your unpublished writing to move your content, be your content, plug your content, or launch someone else's product you use for a fee, and enjoy. That's one other way to launch your unpublished books, booklets, scripts, plays, stories, poems, lyrics, content, or learning material.

Scripts, books, and stories that are unpublished can still find a market on the Web if they are customized to the tastes of those who produce such works. If you have ambition and drive, you could aim to producing your own unpublished direct-to-Web material, called entertainment content.

Your creativity doesn't have to be fiction. It could be learning materials or documentaries. If you don't want to compete with the entertainment industry, there are audiences who want how-to films or videos that were never videos in the first place, but produced direct-to-Web with good multimedia authoring software such as Macromedia's *Director* and other software.

Let your unpublished writing plug, launch, or promote any product you like or a star likes and do it online and on TV. Or package your material with someone else's product. If you're into performing arts, start a Web site for teenagers or any other age group. You can make yourself or anyone else, even a star, spokesperson. The trick is to produce and star in 12-26 half-hour shows aimed at a specific audience, such as teenagers, where you can use your unpublished book to plug the products advertised on the teen magazine Web and/or cable TV show.

You get visibility, publicity, and market your work all at once. If you go for the teen market, produce shows for a Web site, where you'll get to talk honestly with teens about issues they're interested in. Shows can focus in on niche audiences that need Web sites or cable TV teen magazine shows only for them, such as girls from 11-17.

There's one site www.voxxy.com that did that in new ways. If you have a lot of unpublished writing, you want to sell your work in by these two methods: 1. Use a Web site to draw in the stars of TV looking for shows to produce or be spokesperson for. 2. Ask those starts to endorse your writing as they endorse products they enjoy. Find out what they want. Then provide that niche of content, branding, or redemptive value. Keep your idea simple to understand and explain everything clearly in a short paragraph or in one sentence.

The idea of plugging products you like by using your unpublished books and scripts is a form of packaging your books or booklets with products going to be bought. Before the Internet, you'd approach a warehouse or manufacturer and ask that your book be packaged with the products being shipped as a way to give customers a free instructional manual on a product or a sideline, like a cookbook on how to cook with wines or sauces being shipped with packaged wines or sauces.

Now, you do similarly on a Web site, called a Web venture. If you write about baby care, target a Web site for this subject. Observe sites such as www. babystyle.com if you're writing books or booklets about baby wear and care, focus your Web site or content on everything about style and babies. Start your own site focusing on baby style, elder style, teen style, or any other age or other group of interest to parents, women, men, teenage girls, or wherever there is a high demand for information, content, and products.

Women and senior citizens are increasingly on the Web. So you might want to study new *trends* to get a handle on the latest women's interests. Before you get too narrow, pick the audience for the widest possible number of visits to your site. You need to research your markets. Where do people in different targeted groups really want to spend their valuable time visiting?

Find a way to endorse a product or keep asking powerful and popular people to endorse a product that will include your unpublished book along with a product being endorsed as a gift or giveaway. Your content and a manufacturer's product must offer specific benefits and advantages to the buyer.

Use your writing or research to plug someone else's products. If you have an unpublished romance novel, personalize it with the name of the happy couple and package it along with the wedding gifts ordered. Or leave a personalized novel you wrote in guest rooms of hotels with the name of the guests, *if they order it*. Honeymooners might, or it might be of interest to those planning bridal or baby showers, anniversary cruises, or office parties. Always ask the buyer first and show in advance what the product will contain before having anything printed with someone's name.

The quickest way to launch your book is to stage an around the world online launch and media party. Pick a time when most media people are available. Invite the specialty and general press, publishers, agents, entertainment attorneys, producers, directors, book talent managers, book packagers, famous writers, newspaper reporters and columnists. Also invite the members of various public relations and press clubs from your local area chapters.

Include the print media, small press publishers, book sellers, event planners for booksellers events overseas and nationally, and those who come to book sales parties in people's homes. Invite software, book and video distributors to meet you for a conference online where you'll have a chat and put up a presentation with sound, text, and video clips or visuals all about your unpublished book or script.

Did you see the pre release publicity the Harry Potter books received, even coverage on the cover of Newsweek several years ago? What can you do for your unpublished book to create spin that will add to your credibility as well as visibility in the media all over the world?

It all starts with a story board and a press kit that reveals your main character's measured change, transformation, or growth, or if your book's nonfiction, how much everyone needs to know the information you're about to tell. It's not whom you know, but whom you tell—and how you tell it that brings people together. If you want to earn income and cut expenses, you need to be a catalyst.

How Do You Make A Storyboard?

Storyboards can help launch your unpublished book if you use them as a kind of mind map that uses the right hemisphere of the brain to express visually with thumbnail sketches and dialogue bubbles what goes into a novel or script. If you write your story as a play first and flesh out the dialogue into a novel, it will flow easier when based on a storyboard.

You can move to a springboard, where you can bounce the story off of the springboard's role as a summary or synopses of significant events and turning points in your book or script. A springboard runs up to 15 pages long.

A story board can go the length of the book summarizing the highlights in half that number of pages. A synopsis runs about one or two pages, and a high concept pitch is one sentence that tells your whole story such as Star Trek is Wagon Train in space.

What's a storyboard? Storyboards are pages of panel cartoon-like visual images of how a chapter or scene looks visually before the dialogue is spoken. Draw in thumbnail sketches your storyboard for each scene of your novel, autobiography, or script as you write it or adapt it from a novel, news clipping, or story.

To pre sell your unpublished book to the media or publishers, write the significant events, turning points, or highlights of your confrontation where the hero and the opponent come into conflict for the last time. The battle scene is the major test that results in a major change both inside the hero morally and externally so he/she can reach the goal and end the story. This is what you hand to the press and to publishers, agents, or producers. You're highlighting and summarizing the significant events of your book.

1. Hold a mid-night launch party for your life story or other book.

2. Hold a noon launch party for readers who can't drive or go out at night, and have the location near a bus line.

3. Hold a weekend launch party at a department or discount store such as Wal-Mart or any similar store. Or combine with any store's grand opening party.

4. Hold a launch party in a school cafeteria, library, gym, yard, or auditorium for the appropriate age group. Combine launch party with a lecture to elementary or high school classes. Or if more appropriate, to special interest groups and clubs, professional associations, or women's clubs and organizations or related societies.

5. Hold a launch party at a college campus or rent a room or auditorium or space on the lawn.

6. Hold a launch party in a senior citizens apartment complex, recreational center, adult education center, hospital gift shop, or nursing home.

7. Hold a launch party in a place where you can set up an international or national day so that everyone, especially children, if your book is appropriate, can read your book on the same day, in case they do order it. Have all the children across the nation experience *Your Life Story* or *Your Book* on the same day.

8. Hold a launch party in a church recreation hall, park, museum, library, art gallery, zoo, space theater, or social center.

9. Hold a launch party in a mall or on the lawn of a public park or skating rink on a Sunday or at a sports center or field.

10. Hold a launch party on a cruise ship before it sails or in a bus or train station or airport.

Put up a temporary kiosk for your launch party. Or get permission and a permit to launch your book near or in front of a supermarket or convention center or a hotel lobby. Use cruises and travel situations to launch your party. Or charter a flight and launch it in transit to help passengers pass the time. Cruise ships are you best bet.

Ask newspaper reporters from national press associations and public relations associations to cover your book or life story in their articles on lifestyle or business subjects or whatever the subject of your book covers. Societies of professional journalists have monthly meetings. Ask to have your launch party at one of their meetings or invite the whole organization to your meeting.

Gather other writers of similar books and life stories into a pool of vendors and sell booths or tables in a large hall, Masonic center, or other meeting place, like an association of Realtor's Hall, or building you can rent. Have all the writers self-publish their books or photocopy with cardstock cover and illustration or photo and comb binding. Print on demand.

Have numerous copies of books on tables. A group of 10 or 20 writers can have a group launch party and invite the press or sponsor a press club meeting, perhaps on board a docked yacht that's rented for the day or in a hotel or university rented room or meeting hall. Books can be printed on demand and given as press copies to reporters.

Invite entertainment and copyright attorneys, agents, publishers, editors, the media, and writers, also the potential readers of your book such as children and parents or business people. Have your launch party at a convention or conference on a related theme, such as a conference of small press publishers or a book buyer's convention or annual meeting in the US or abroad. Or take a group of writers on a cruise and present books to the press.

You can go free if you gather enough paying people to take the tour with you. Have stationery printed with a logo or slogan. Print the letterhead with enlarged slogan or logo onto a supply of two-pocket folders. Print a scriptwriting logo onto adhesive labels. Stick the labels onto the cover of the folders. The multi-colored two-pocket folders are available in any office supply outlet.

Create a brochure, preferably in color. Include the brochure in the press kit. Make an electronic media kit as well as a print press kit. The brochure could list a writer's services and credentials or credits. If there are no past credits, print all the services provided such as the following:

1.   Quality circles for writers

2.   Individual instruction

3.   Seminars, event planning for communications professionals

4. Freelance technical writing, manual writing, corporate scriptwriting, desktop publishing, word processing, editing, tutoring, instructional courseware design, children's writing instruction, corporate scriptwriting

5. English as a second language writing instruction

6. Fiction written for adults with 2nd grade reading ability

7. Science journalism

8. Writer's speakers bureau

9. Art

10. Publicity writing, or any other type of writing services offered.

Nourishment is a Fountain

What's your most powerful resource you can call on when you need it? It is not only the source within, but the source without also. How do you write about this source? How can you use this source to both cut expenses and bring in income while expanding your creative abilities? Nourishment is all about offering the public and the media positive magnets. Decades ago these magnets or catalysts were called positive hooks because they hooked the readers or viewers. You had a captured audience.

The idea behind nourishment or positive incentives is that people don't want a steady diet of pain, fear, and horror—all the time. If they did, then books such as the *Chicken Soup* series would come in second place to gladiatorial blood sport movies. Nourishment sells. There is a market for joy. Don't dump pain on readers all the way through your writing—not if you are writing for a large audience.

People buy audio books, videos, learning materials, and information books to learn more about health, mind, spirit, investments, or contemporary culture issues. Which sells more books or videos—works about poverty or the habits of billionaires?

The habits of billionaires and efficient people are of more interest than documentaries and books on poverty. Why don't enough people buy books surveying the plight of those in poverty or pain? The media will help you launch your work if you provide solutions to problems and results. Offer easy and quick solutions backed up by detailed step-by-step information people can follow.

Large audiences want to hear about the secrets of healing, love, wealth, and happiness. Nourishment sells along with commitment and inspiration. People also want to improve their memory, enhance creativity, and be happy. Instruction is in high demand. People want instructions that they can easily understand. They want to know how to build, make, or repair an object. Most people have little time or money to spend on luxuries.

Look at the success of home improvement centers. Those with time to "build it at home" want to create a device better in quality, safer, and at lower cost than can be bought commercially. An example would be instructions on how to make your own shampoo from scratch. With home-made shampoo, you could customize a non-toxic formula for your own hair's needs using natural flower essences, oils, moisturizes, scents, or spices. People are looking for safer hair tints, depilatories, and other products that are absorbed by the pores. That's why you need a professional-looking electronic and portfolio-type print media kit.

Whatever your creative project entails, include a press kit when giving presentations, seminars, interviews, radio or T.V. appearances or querying editors, producers, publishers, agents, and entertainment attorneys. Send the press kit to newspaper and magazine editors, television producers, and radio talk show hosts seeking guests from the writing community. Even mystery and suspense novels or true crime accounts have to offer more than violence and justice.

The purpose of a press kit is to inform people that scriptwriting is being done on a full-time basis and assignments are wanted either re-writing other writer's scripts or created fiction or non-fiction video and film scripts for production. Industrial video and the trade magazines are constant users of video scripts for training.

Media kits, also called press kits are included in presentations, pitching, written proposals, sales packets, query letters, and in general correspondence. Marketing and sales for home-based scriptwriters are fields worth writing about in print and in training video script format.

33

How Do You Create A Powerful Media Magnet?

Every scriptwriter needs an online press kit to pre-sell a script to the video or film market. Most print press kits are discarded by the media without being opened, unless you're well-known. The only way the media will pay attention to a press kit is if it contains a powerful hook. Have one sentence or question that will repeat at the beginning, middle, and end of the press kit. Bring the media to your Web site before you mail out expensive printed material to someone who doesn't contact you and ask for a review copy or press kit of your work.

Use a question hook that makes a busy editor stop and think. Make the question personal and universal. Put on the press kit's cover a hook question that makes the media do some introverted thinking. In large type letters have the question make an impact. You can ask the reader to name his or her strongest source. In the past, media kits used words like "powerful resource" or "strongest magnet."

Notice that that question that holds the reader's attention is the same as the one you ask of your hero when creating a screenplay, novel, or short story. Another powerful hook question that has been used in media press kits and in presentations to the press in the past is, "How many times have you sold out on your real dreams and settled for something less?" However, today, this type of question might get a response like, "None of your business." So use something that makes your content more *approachable* such as "You don't have to settle for reality anymore. Your dreams just woke up your imagination."

You want the reader in the media to feel important and good about himself while reading your press kit. You want to nourish the press. You don't want to frighten, shock, or remind the reader of human mortality or frailty. Media kits are there to make you likeable.

Use a statement instead of a question to draw the reader in. Questions often bring knee-jerk hostility responses. Soothe the reader. Put the statement on the cover of your press kit folder and also inside the press release.

If you want to launch anything in the media, you need to show commitment and credibility. You're a media strategist, an architect and designer of 'models' on paper that create visibility in the media for your unsold, pre-sold, or in-development content or product.

In the middle of the press release, exert power. Write about how the reader can do something to increase his or her power. You could show the reader what one act he or she could perform to become more powerful. Don't ask a question in the middle of your press release.

A question wastes the limited time available, usually 20 seconds spent to read a one-page media release. Instead, illustrate in words how to solve a problem, obtain a result, or get more powerful by performing one act. That one act would directly relate to your product, premise, or content. In one sentence, tell the reader exactly what he or she has to do to become more powerful. That's the selling point of your item.

Professional-looking press kits publicize any item inexpensively. Paid advertising would cost hundreds of dollars for a two-inch display ad in daily newspaper or high-circulation trade journal.

A press kit is an open invitation for the writer to be hired by colleges of extended studies at $50 an hour or 50% of the gross of student's fees to give a one-day seminar on writing. Experience is more important than a degree at such adult education seminars in private schools. Exposure, such as giving seminars for producers and directors on script analysis and consulting, leads to better chances to have personal screenplays seen by producers.

Stop using fear as an advertisement to draw in people. There are enough ads on TV that start with a screeching ambulance or loud, fast heartbeats, screams, or a man shouting how he's dying or crying. These ads often are broadcast after midnight or late at night, when most frail seniors are up watching TV and just dozing off. It shocks people out of sleep, particularly the frail elderly or people with disabilities who are not able to sleep easily.

So if you fell asleep in front of your TV set, these types of ads may shock you out of your sweet dream with fearful possible reality scenarios that remind you of your mortality, pain, or diseases. The shock ads are there to get you to buy safety products. Older people feel anxiety when such ads come on. It reminds them of what's ahead. Instead of making them think about preparing for possible events or their final expenses, people sometimes are shocked awake into a panic attack or worse by the sudden noise of screaming sirens and shouting or loud rapidly beating sounds. Shock ads are unwelcome by those with panic disorder or sensitized nervous systems.

What ads do seniors like? Serenity is one. You can sell serenity to the media. Instead of wondering how many people get sick watching other people getting sick, use the opposite to attract attention. Offer gently bubbling fountains, quiet rivers and sunsets, beaches, mountains, pine trees, gardens, and anything that brings joy and contentment in TV ads that appear in the wee hours of the night.

To promote a product, use "two word" titles. Or use the word "Why" in your title if you're giving information. For nonfiction, use an insightful, popular, and commercial short two-word title such as "Robot Cowboys" Or a trendy title that tells the whole story of the nonfiction book: "Why Writers Want More Monies and Publishers Want More Funnies." Or "Why Women Want More_(drama)____and Men Want More_(sports)____"

What Do Media Professionals Expect To See in a Media Kit?

Newspaper and magazine editors, radio and T.V. producers, agents, publicists, entertainment attorneys, directors, actors, film, and video creative directors are used to receiving professionally printed press kits. They only read material sent in an "acceptable format."

An acceptable press kit consists of a double-pocketed file folder, the question hook printed on the cover (not typed on a regular typewriter, but typeset with desktop publishing fonts). Inside the flap pocket is another question hook on the inside cover. In the flap-pocket is a black and white glossy photo of the writer (matte for television producers).

On top of the photo is a four-page press release about what the writer has to offer that needs visibility—and how the information will help the community or readers. A short, one-page press release goes on top of the four-page release. The short press release gives the writer's biography, credits, credentials, and anything else important the writer has done in relation to what the longer press release covers.

News clippings about the writer or the script are put over the short press release. The clippings are cut out, dated, titled, and pasted on a sheet of paper and then photocopied onto a slick, camera-ready white sheet. Include in the second flap pocket a copy of any article, booklet, book, sample, or tape for media review. This press kit goes to agents as well as media editors and producers. Make sure you have an electric press kit on a Web site and also sent to the media as well as print folders. Too many paper print media kit folders are thrown away or recy-

cled without being read. No one is paying anyone to read media kits sent unsolicited, and there's very little time to read them. The exception would be those on a
newspaper staff paid to write book reviews or producers that book radio and TV
authors as guests on programs.

What does a press kit pitch? Place a two-page pitch release on top of all the
other information in the kit tells the media why the script is so extraordinary, so
unique and different and who can benefit by seeing it. Include a marketability
study of who would be buying the script, book, or tape. The new age video market is on the rise.

On top of every release, place the final cover letter as a courtesy, telling why
you want the media to print selected press releases and the photo inside. The
cover letter is one page or less in length. The first paragraph of the cover letter
contains a premise—of the release. What's important is summarized in one sentence.

Use concrete credentials that can be checked. If the press kit is going to a publisher to sell a book/script package deal, include a chapter breakdown. The titles
of the chapters sell the book just as the title of a video script determines its commercial appeal.

Book chapter summaries vary from three paragraphs to under a page for highlights. Tell the media exactly what viewers will be told when they view the script.
For script/booklet combinations such as book and audio tape combinations, or
video and instructional manual packages, write down the components of the
book in a press kit, and send a sample. This technique holds true for self-published and self-produced video/book packages used for instruction or motivation.

The first chapter of a book is like the first scene of a video script. It's the selling chapter. In a media kit designed to sell and outline a book and video package,
tell the reader why she needs to read the book and view the video. Include photos
or a mock-up copy of the video or book combination.

The fastest way to impress a reader about a video is to have an advertisement
or poster with a black background and white print. The print is superimposed
over a photo in the background. Viewers will remember that video above one on
a white background with black lettering and design.

It's possible to create an infomercial to mail out to potential buyers who might
be interested in purchasing a produced video or a published book, but it's expensive. A press kit creating visibility for a video, a script, or a book is more direct.
Use one sentence to summarize your book, pamphlet, article, or script's premise.

Marketing researchers often report that readers will respond faster to an article
written by a reporter about a person, business, or product than to a paid adver-

tisement placed by the entrepreneur. An article I wrote for a high-circulation paper brought in 600 requests for information when I included my post office box number. The tiny, classified ad I placed in the back of the paper (which was expensive for me) brought no responses.

Visibility influences marketing. Contacts with video software distributors lead to contacts with producers. A commercial title can pre-sell a script. Free publicity and press coverage pulls more weight than small, paid display ads announcing "script for sale." Press coverage is free, and can be obtained by a phone call and a news angle or a press kit.

34

Reunions

How to Startup A Family Reunions Business on the Internet, or Satellite for Videoconferencing

DESCRIPTION OF BUSINESS:

You can bring long-separated family members together even though each member may live in a different corner of the globe by creating video reunions. Similar videos can be created for retired military, school and college alumni, and other long-separated friends and co-workers.

INCOME POTENTIAL:

For a small fee—the cost of taping plus a margin of profit, a few dollars per minute, plus a little more than the cost of each copy of the videotape, you can unite families on the Internet, by video or videoconferencing, and give each family member a copy of the family reunion tape.

Back in 1994, the cost came out to about $4 a minute to reunite people on television through a hookup to a satellite. One company, *Canal Uno*, helped to unite families or hold business videoconferences.

Today, you can charge sliding scale fees for family members, refugees, retired military, co-workers, school alumni, missing persons, or the physically ill, depending on the budget, your cost, and the ability to pay of the client. Your goal is to bring together people long separated for a reunion on tape because none of the members could come in person due to financial inability, distance, work obligations, age, or illness.

BEST LOCALE TO OPERATE THE BUSINESS:

Locate anywhere there are large populations of immigrants and refugees, or anywhere your target populations congregate. You will be linking together people at a distance by video and phone.

On the video will be relatives, friends, co-workers, immigrants, refugees, or former soldiers who now live anywhere in the world. These people may not have seen their relatives and friends for decades. What they all have in common is that they want a reunion on non-broadcast television.

TRAINING REQUIRED:

You'll need to know how to operate your camcorder and television videoconferencing equipment. Or work with Internet connections. If you can't afford to buy satellite time, then you can limit your service to putting family reunions on DVDs or on the Web or other Internet arrangement, or plan videoconferencing with the client footing the bill for any satellite hookup.

Recommended are books or a course on how to produce with your video camera and how to produce videoconferences using satellite hookups. Contact the satellite companies for training offers or inquire in the telecommunications department of your local community college.

GENERAL APTITUDE OR EXPERIENCE:

You'll need to stand on your feet a lot and operate a camera. You should learn how to hook up television cables and devices. The best experience is hands-on volunteering with other small producers. Experience can be gained by joining professional associations related to video or satellites and volunteer to be on their teams or get available short and low-cost training offered by the business associations. Attend or volunteer to help out at conventions and conferences.

VIDEO EQUIPMENT NEEDED:

You'll need a telephone line open to whatever countries you're hooking up to as well as a satellite connection. Your office can be in your home or in a small building. You'll need a room or studio to operate in or space to put your television screen and camera. A home office or garage can be used for your equipment. Perhaps a spare bedroom can be outfitted with camcorders and computers.

OPERATING YOUR BUSINESS:

Expect the reunions to be emotional. You could create a high-tech video network in a small building that brings families together from a part of the world you choose.

You are allowing families to be close for a short time on television. Seat relatives in a small room with a big television camera mounted in the back wall.

Here's one example from the mid-nineties. Canal Uno (Channel One) debuted on January 15, 1994. It provided the technology for families to talk to each member instantaneously on television, usually for 20 minutes. By satellite connection, each family member talked and viewed one another on a television screen.

If you start your own reunion business at home to make spare cash or to cut your own expenses, your reunions can last for what ever time slot you make—20 minutes—for example, depending upon the time you're allowed to use. You can work with the Internet or where there is no Internet connection, a satellite connection.

To look back at the Canal Uno example of 1994, El Salvadorans in Texas, California, Maryland, New Jersey, Washington, D.C., Virginia, and Florida could use this high-tech link to Central America. Canal Uno, in June 1994, handled about 100 links a week between the United States and El Salvador.

The courier firm, Gigante Express' opened back in 1983 when a young El Salvadoran entrepreneur, Jose Carlos Perez Saleh, had a plan to bring Canal Uno to Nicaragua, Honduras and Guatemala.

Before Canal Uno began operating, Gigante Express carried 30,000 letters a week as a major courier service from the firm's 52 offices in the United States and Canada to El Salvador, Nicaragua, Honduras and Guatemala.

This is one example of how successful high technology can be when applied to bringing people together or acting as a courier service. Gigante as the first Central American courier company soon became the largest of more than 100 courier companies in El Salvador. How does this success case history apply to you at home?

You, too, as a family reunion video producer, also can make use of any type of technology that's affordable—from broadband Internet connections to satellite hookups feeding into your camcorder, monitor, or TV set. Your goal would be to bring long-separated people together and give them discs of their family members or long-lost friends anywhere in the world.

As a sideline, you can also do videoconferencing for corporation executives who need to attend interviews, seminars, and meetings around the globe without the bother and expense of jet lag.

Particularly in demand are satellite hookups to the Pacific Rim nations such as Japan, China, Taiwan, the Philippines, and Australia with the rest of the Far East linked to the West Coast of the United States for executive merger and business talk.

TARGET MARKET:

If you find out how many thousands of people from specific countries live in your area, you'll be able to estimate your target market. How many people from a given country live in the city you're in today?

Work with population demographics. Your goal is to reach interested people to make the distance between their old country and their new homeland seem smaller through the use of the home camcorder, wireless Internet, phone lines, or a satellite hookup.

Also contact realtors, vacation housing exchange firms, travel agents, and tour guides as well as executives at Fortune 500 companies to see whether they would like your videoconferencing services.

Reunions are not only for long-separated family members. They can be for business executives from around the world who need to connect via satellite and video.

RELATED VIDEO OPPORTUNITIES:

You can use your satellite time slot to broadcast election returns from foreign countries and tape them for distribution to community members or researchers. Team up with persons who speak foreign languages, Track how many people from the various countries live in your area and research what their needs are and what type of reunions would interest them. Cater to their videoconferencing needs by Internet, satellite hookup, camcorder, and DVDs or other compact discs.

ADDITIONAL INFORMATION:

International Teleconferencing Association
1150 Connecticut Ave NW, Ste. 1050
Washington, DC 20036

Satellite Video Exchange Society
1102 Homer St.
Vancouver, BC Canada V6B 2X6

Satellite Broadcasting & Communications Association
225 Reinekers Lane
Station 600
Alexandria, VA 22314

International Association of Satellite Users
PO Box DD
6845 Elm St.
McLean, VA 22101

Society for Private and Commercial Earth Stations
c/o Richard L. Brown
1920 N St. NW
Washington, DC 20036

Society of Telecommunications Consultants
One Rockefeller Plaza, Suite 1912
New York, NY 10020

Envirovideos
PO Box 629000
El Dorado Hills, CA 95762

El Salvador Media Project
335 W. 38th St., 5th fl.
New York, NY 10018

35

Scrap Booking Skits: Personal History Keepsakes & Time Capsules

Turn oral or personal history significant events and life story highlights into 45-minute one-act plays for student audiences. Skits and plays are *time capsules* that can be included with family history and genealogy keepsakes. Record and transcribe the skits, monologues, life stories, oral histories, or plays.

Here are the steps you need to take in order to gather life story highlights to turn into skits, plays, monologues, vignettes, or other time capsules for high-school, college, or junior-high student audiences. Anything recorded needs to have a text transcription in case the technology advances and the recording medium disappears before the material can be transferred to a newer medium.

Examples would be records made for Victrolas or phonographs would not be able to play on current DVD players. If one generation forgets to transfer the time capsule from video tape or DVD to the next technology, at least photos and transcribed text would be viewable.

Use the following sequence when gathering oral/aural histories:

1. Develop one central issue and divide that issue into a few important questions that highlight or focus on that one central issue.

2. Write out a plan just like a business plan for your oral history project. You may have to use that plan later to ask for a grant for funding, if required. Make a list of all your products that will result from the oral history when it's done.

3. Write out a plan for publicity or public relations and media relations. How are you going to get the message to the public or special audiences?

4. Develop a budget. This is important if you want a grant or to see how much you'll have to spend on creating an oral history project.

5. List the cost of video taping and editing, packaging, publicity, and help with audio or special effects and stock shot photos of required.

6. What kind of equipment will you need? List that and the time slots you give to each part of the project. How much time is available? What are your deadlines?

7. What's your plan for a research? How are you going to approach the people to get the interviews? What questions will you ask?

8. Do the interviews. Arrive prepared with a list of questions. It's okay to ask the people the kind of questions they would like to be asked. Know what dates the interviews will cover in terms of time. Are you covering the economic depression of the thirties? World Wars? Fifties? Sixties? Pick the time parameters.

9. Edit the interviews so you get the highlights of experiences and events, the important parts. Make sure what's important to you also is important to the person you interviewed.

10. Find out what the interviewee wants to emphasize perhaps to highlight events in a life story. Create a video-biography of the highlights of one person's life or an oral history of an event or series of events.

11. Process audio as well as video, and make sure you have written transcripts of anything on audio and/or video in case the technology changes or the tapes go bad.

12. Save the tapes to compact disks, DVDs, a computer hard disk and several other ways to preserve your oral history time capsule. Donate any tapes or CDs to appropriate archives, museums, relatives of the interviewee, and one or more oral history libraries. They are usually found at universities that have an oral history department and library such as UC Berkeley and others.

13. Check the Web for oral history libraries at universities in various states and abroad.

14. Evaluate what you have edited. Make sure the central issue and central questions have been covered in the interview. Find out whether newspa-

pers or magazines want summarized transcripts of the audio and/or video with photos.

15. Contact libraries, archives, university oral history departments and relevant associations and various ethnic genealogy societies that focus on the subject matter of your central topic.

16. Keep organizing what you have until you have long and short versions of your oral history for various archives and publications. Contact magazines and newspapers to see whether editors would assign reporters to do a story on the oral history project.

17. Create a scrapbook with photos and summarized oral histories. Write a synopsis of each oral history on a central topic or issue. Have speakers give public presentations of what you have for each person interviewed and/or for the entire project using highlights of several interviews with the media for publicity. Be sure your project is archived properly and stored in a place devoted to oral history archives and available to researchers and authors.

Aural/Oral History Techniques

1. Begin with easy to answer questions that don't require you explore and probe deeply in your first question. Focus on one central issue when asking questions. Don't use abstract questions. A plain question would be "What's your purpose?" An abstract question with connotations would be "What's your crusade?" Use questions with denotations instead of connotations. Keep questions short and plain—easy to understand. Examples would be, "What did you want to accomplish? How did you solve those problems? How did you find closure?" Ask the familiar "what, when, who, where, how, and why."

2. First research written or visual resources before you begin to seek an oral history of a central issue, experience, or event.

3. Who is your intended audience?

4. What kind of population niche or sample will you target?

5. What means will you select to choose who you will interview? What group of people will be central to your interview?

6. Write down how you'll explain your project. Have a script ready so you don't digress or forget what to say on your feet.

7. Consult oral history professionals if you need more information. Make sure what you write in your script will be clear to understand by your intended audience.

8. Have all the equipment you need ready and keep a list of what you'll use and the cost. Work up your budget.

9. Choose what kind of recording device is best—video, audio, multimedia, photos, and text transcript. Make sure your video is broadcast quality. I use a Sony Digital eight (high eight) camera.

10. Make sure from cable TV stations or news stations that what type of video and audio you choose ahead of time is broadcast quality.

11. Make sure you have an external microphone and also a second microphone as a second person also tapes the interview in case the quality of your camera breaks down. You can also keep a tape recorder going to capture the audio in case your battery dies.

12. Make sure your battery is fully charged right before the interview. Many batteries die down after a day or two of nonuse.

13. Test all equipment before the interview and before you leave your office or home. I've had batteries go down unexpectedly and happy there was another person ready with another video camera waiting and also an audio tape version going.

14. Make sure the equipment works if it's raining, hot, cold, or other weather variations. Test it before the interview. Practice interviewing someone on your equipment several times to get the hang of it before you show up at the interview.

15. Make up your mind how long the interview will go before a break and use tape of that length, so you have one tape for each segment of the interview. Make several copies of your interview questions.

16. Be sure the interviewee has a copy of the questions long before the interview so the person can practice answering the questions and think of what to say or even take notes. Keep checking your list of what you need to do.

17. Let the interviewee make up his own questions if he wants. Perhaps your questions miss the point. Present your questions first. Then let him embellish the questions or change them as he wants to fit the central issue with his own experiences.

18. Call the person two days and then one day before the interview to make sure the individual will be there on time and understands how to travel to the location. Or if you are going to the person's home, make sure you understand how to get there.

19. Allow yourself one extra hour in case of traffic jams.

20. Choose a quiet place. Turn off cell phones and any ringing noises. Make sure you are away from barking dogs, street noise, and other distractions.

21. Before you interview make sure the person knows he or she is going to be video and audio-taped.

22. If you don't want anyone swearing, make that clear it's for public archives and perhaps broadcast to families.

23. Your interview questions should follow the journalist's information-seeking format of asking, who, what, where, where, how, and why. Oral history is a branch of journalistic research.

24. Let the person talk and don't interrupt. You be the listener and think of oral history as aural history from your perspective.

25. Make sure only one person speaks without being interrupted before someone else takes his turn to speak.

26. Understand silent pauses are for thinking of what to say.

27. Ask one question and let the person gather his thoughts.

28. Finish all your research on one question before jumping to the next question. Keep it organized by not jumping back to the first question after the second is done. Stay in a linear format.

29. Follow up what you can about any one question, finish with it, and move on to the next question without circling back. Focus on listening instead of asking rapid fire questions as they would confuse the speaker.

30. Ask questions that allow the speaker to begin to give a story, anecdote, life experience, or opinion along with facts. Don't ask questions that can be answered only be yes or no. This is not a courtroom. Let the speaker elaborate with facts and feelings or thoughts.

31. Late in the interview, start to ask questions that explore and probe for deeper answers.

32. Wrap up with how the person solved the problem, achieved results, reached a conclusion, or developed an attitude, or found the answer. Keep the wrap-up on a light, uplifting note.

33. Don't leave the individual hanging in emotion after any intensity of. Respect the feelings and opinions of the person. He or she may see the situation from a different point of view than someone else. So respect the person's right to feel as he does. Respect his need to recollect his own experiences.

34. Interview for only one hour at a time. If you have only one chance, interview for an hour. Take a few minutes break. Then interview for the second hour. Don't interview more than two hours at any one meeting.

35. Use prompts such as paintings, photos, music, video, diaries, vintage clothing, crafts, antiques, or memorabilia when appropriate. Carry the photos in labeled files or envelopes to show at appropriate times in order to prime the memory of the interviewee. For example, you may show a childhood photo and ask "What was it like in that orphanage where these pictures were taken?" Or travel photos might suggest a trip to America as a child, or whatever the photo suggests. For example, "Do you remember when this ice cream parlor inside the ABC movie house stood at the corner of X and Y Street? Did you go there as a teenager? What was your funniest memory of this movie theater or the ice cream store inside back in the fifties?"

36. As soon as the interview is over, label all the tapes and put the numbers in order.

37. A signed release form is required before you can broadcast anything. So have the interviewee sign a release form before the interview.

38. Make sure the interviewee gets a copy of the tape and a transcript of what he or she said on tape. If the person insists on making corrections,

send the paper transcript of the tape for correction to the interviewee. Edit the tape as best you can or have it edited professionally.

39. Make sure you comply with all the corrections the interviewee wants changed. He or she may have given inaccurate facts that need to be corrected on the paper transcript.

40. Have the tape edited with the corrections, even if you have to make a tape at the end of the interviewee putting in the corrections that couldn't be edited out or changed.

41. As a last resort, have the interviewee redo the part of the tape that needs correction and have it edited in the tape at the correct place marked on the tape. Keep the paper transcript accurate and up to date, signed with a release form by the interviewee.

42. Oral historians write a journal of field notes about each interview. Make sure these get saved and archived so they can be read with the transcript.

43. Have the field notes go into a computer where someone can read them along with the transcript of the oral history tape or CD.

44. Thank the interviewee in writing for taking the time to do an interview for broadcast and transcript.

45. Put a label on everything you do from the interview to the field notes. Make a file and sub file folders and have everything stored in a computer, in archived storage, and in paper transcript.

46. Make copies and digital copies of all photos and put into the records in a computer. Return originals to owners.

47. Make sure you keep your fingerprints off the photos by wearing white cotton gloves. Use cardboard when sending the photos back and pack securely. Also photocopy the photos and scan the photos into your computer. Treat photos as antique art history in preservation.

48. Make copies for yourself of all photos, tapes, and transcripts. Use your duplicates, and store the original as the master tape in a place that won't be used often, such as a time capsule or safe, or return to a library or museum where the original belongs.

49. Return all original photos to the owners. An oral history archive library or museum also is suitable for original tapes. Use copies only to work from, copy, or distribute.

50. Index your tapes and transcripts. To use oral history library and museum terminology, recordings and transcripts are given "accession numbers."

51. Phone a librarian in an oral history library of a university for directions on how to assign accession numbers to your tapes and transcripts if the materials are going to be stored at that particular library. Store copies in separate places in case of loss or damage.

52. If you don't know where the materials will be stored, use generic accession numbers to label your tapes and transcripts. Always keep copies available for yourself in case you have to duplicate the tapes to send to an institution, museum, or library, or to a broadcast company.

53. Make synopses available to public broadcasting radio and TV stations.

54. Check your facts.

55. Are you missing anything you want to include?

56. Is there some place you want to send these tapes and transcripts such as an ethnic museum, radio show, or TV satellite station specializing in the topics on the tapes, such as public TV stations? Would it be suitable for a world music station? A documentary station?

57. If you need more interviews, arrange them if possible.

58. Give the interviewee a copy of the finished product with the corrections. Make sure the interviewee signs a release form that he or she is satisfied with the corrections and is releasing the tape to you and your project.

59. Store the tapes and transcripts in a library or museum or at a university or other public place where it will be maintained and preserved for many generations and restored when necessary.

60. You can also send copies to a film repository or film library that takes video tapes, an archive for radio or audio tapes for radio broadcast or cable TV.

61. Copies may be sent to various archives for storage that lasts for many generations. Always ask whether there are facilities for restoring the tape.

A museum would most likely have these provisions as would a large library that has an oral history library project or section.

62. Make sure the master copy is well protected and set up for long-term storage in a place where it will be protected and preserved.

63. If the oral history is about events in history, various network news TV stations might be interested. Film stock companies may be interested in copies of old photos.

64. Find out from the subject matter what type of archives, repository, or storage museums and libraries would be interested in receiving copies of the oral history tapes and transcripts.

Print media libraries would be interested in the hard paper copy transcripts and photos as would various ethnic associations and historical preservation societies. Find out whether the materials will go to microfiche, film, or be digitized and put on CDs and DVDs, or on the World Wide Web. If you want to create a time capsule for the Web, you can ask the interviewee whether he or she wants the materials or selected materials to be put online or on CD as multimedia or other. Then you would get a signed release from the interviewee authorizing you to put the materials or excerpts online. Also find out in whose name the materials are copyrighted and whether you have print and electronic rights to the material or do the owners-authors-interviewees—or you, the videographer-producer? Get it all in writing, signed by those who have given you any interviews, even if you have to call your local intellectual property rights attorney

How Accurate Are Autobiographies, Biographies, Personal Histories, Plays and Monologues Based on Life Stories?

Autobiographies, biographies, personal histories, plays, and monologues present a point of view. Are all sides given equal emphasis? Will the audience choose favorite characters? Cameras give fragments, points of view, and bits and pieces. Viewers will see what the videographer or photographer intends to be seen. The interviewee will also be trying to put his point of view across and tell the story from his perspective.

Will the photographer or videographer be in agreement with the interviewee? Or if you are recording for print transcript, will your point of view agree with the interviewee's perspective and experience if your basic 'premise,' where you two are coming from, are not in agreement? Think this over as you write your list of questions. Do both of you agree on your central issue on which you'll focus for the interview?

How are you going to turn spoken words into text for your paper hard copy transcript? Will you transcribe verbatim, correct the grammar, or quote as you hear the spoken words? Oral historians really need to transcribe the exact spoken word. You can leave out the 'ahs' and 'oms' or loud pauses, as the interviewee thinks what to say next. You don't want to sound like a court reporter, but you do want to have an accurate record transcribed of what was spoken.

You're also not editing for a movie, unless you have permission to turn the oral history into a TV broadcast, where a lot gets cut out of the interview for time constraints. For that, you'd need written permission so words won't be taken out of context and strung together in the editing room to say something different from what the interviewee intended to say.

Someone talking could put in wrong names, forget what they wanted to say, or repeat themselves. They could mumble, ramble, or do almost anything. So you would have to sit down and weed out redundancy when you can or decide on presenting exactly what you've heard as transcript.

When someone reads the transcript in text, they won't have what you had in front of you, and they didn't see and hear the live presentation or the videotape. It's possible to misinterpret gestures or how something is spoken, the mood or tone, when reading a text transcript. Examine all your sources. Use an ice-breaker to get someone talking.

If a woman is talking about female-interest issues, she may feel more comfortable talking to another woman. Find out whether the interviewee is more comfortable speaking to someone of his or her own age. Some older persons feel they can relate better to someone close to their own age than someone in high school, but it varies. Sometimes older people can speak more freely to a teenager.

The interviewee must be able to feel comfortable with the interviewer and know he or she will not be judged. Sometimes it helps if the interviewer is the same ethnic group or there is someone present of the same group or if new to the language, a translator is present.

Read some books on oral history field techniques. Read the National Genealogical Society Quarterly (NGSQ). Also look at The American Genealogist (TAG), The Genealogist, and The New England Historical and Genealogical Register (The Register). If you don't know the maiden name of say, your grandmother's mother, and no relative knows either because it wasn't on her death certificate, try to reconstruct the lives of the males who had ever met the woman whose maiden name is unknown.

Maybe she did business with someone before marriage or went to school or court. Someone may have recorded the person's maiden name before her marriage. Try medical records if any were kept. There was no way to find my mother's grandmother's maiden name until I started searching to see whether she had any brothers in this country. She had to have come as a passenger on a ship around 1880 as she bought a farm. Did her husband come with her?

Was the farm in his name? How many brothers did she have in this country with her maiden surname? If the brothers were not in this country, what countries did they come from and what cities did they live in before they bought the farm in Albany? If I could find out what my great grandmother's maiden name was through any brothers living at the time, I could contact their descendants perhaps and see whether any male or female lines are still in this country or where else on the globe.

Perhaps a list of midwives in the village at the time is recorded in a church or training school for midwives. Fix the person in time and place. Find out whom she might have done business with and whether any records of that business exist. What businesses did she patronize? Look for divorce or court records, change of name records, and other legal documents.

Look at local sources. Did anyone save records from bills of sale for weddings, purchases of homes, furniture, debutante parties, infant supplies, or even medical records? Look at nurses' licenses, midwives' registers, employment contracts, and teachers' contracts, alumni associations for various schools, passports, passenger lists, alien registration cards, naturalization records, immigrant aid societies, city directories, and cross-references.

Try religious and women's clubs, lineage and village societies, girl scouts and similar groups, orphanages, sanatoriums, hospitals, police records. Years ago there was even a Eugenics Record Office. What about the women's prisons? The first one opened in 1839—Mount Pleasant Female Prison, NY.

Try voters' lists. If your relative is from another country, try records in those villages or cities abroad. Who kept the person's diaries? Have you checked the Orphan Train records? Try ethnic and religious societies and genealogy associations for that country. Most ethnic genealogy societies have a special interest group for even the smallest villages in various countries.

You can start one and put up a Web site for people who also come from there in past centuries. Check alimony, divorce, and court records, widow's pensions of veterans, adoptions, orphanages, foster homes, medical records, birth, marriage, and death certificates, social security, immigration, pet license owners' files, prisons, alumni groups from schools, passenger lists, military, and other legal records.

When all historical records are being tied together, you can add the DNA testing to link all those cousins. Check military pensions on microfilms in the National Archives. See the bibliography section of this book for further resources on highly recommended books and articles on oral history field techniques and similar historical subjects.

36

Shampoo

Glycerin added to shampoo adds a softer touch to the hair. Buy glycerin from your pharmacy. Make your own shampoo customized to your individual hair needs. Check out the various Web sites with recipes on them for making your own shampoo. The Garden Web site at http://forums2.gardenweb.com/forums/load/herbal/msg0206441320821.html has some recipes for making shampoos. How do you make your own shampoo? Start with basic ingredients and decide whether you want to make dog shampoo or shampoo for humans. Here's how to make dog shampoo.

Dog Shampoo

Mix together: One pint of very gentle non-scented dishwashing liquid without added coloring such as Dove or Ivory dishwashing liquid. Add one pint of distilled water, one pint of room temperature apple cider vinegar, and four ounces of glycerin. Mix together all ingredients and use up immediately. Don't store it as it biodegrades quickly or spoils like food. See this or a similar recipe for dog shampoo at the Homemade Dog Shampoo Web site at http://www.abigslice.com/shampup.html. You'll also find recipes for homemade products at the Recipe Bazaar at: http://www.recipezaar.com/mycookbook/book/30594. For my own dog shampoo, I like to mix three ounces of glycerin from a pharmacy with a pint of water and add ¼ cup of white distilled vinegar. To this I add a cup of orange blossom (petals) water. I use my water distiller to boil rose petals or orange blossom petals and make distilled water with a flower scent. However, for doggie shampoo, all you really need is a mixture of water, a little vinegar, and glycerin with a very mild, clear, non-scented dishwashing liquid that's gentle to the hands.

Sometimes I make chamomile tea and mix the weak chamomile tea—about two teabags to two quarts of water with some mild dishwashing soap and four ounces of glycerin mixed with a quarter cup of vinegar. I let everything cool to room temperature and use this as a dog shampoo. Always ask your veterinarian before you mix any ingredients to make dog shampoo to make sure it's suitable for a dog's skin.

Check out the Recipe for Dog Soap for dry skin at: http://www. soapmakingsecrets.com/soapmaking/recipe-for-dog-soap-for-dry-skin-.asp. The site also asks whether you want to make soap and also want to run a thriving business. One way to work at home is to make soap for dogs with dry skin or customized soaps for humans or pets. So look at the various Web sites online that offer recipes for making shampoos and soaps for humans or pets. Do your research and homework. Find out what consumers say about recipes on any Web site. There is a wealth of information at this site.

Shampoo for Humans

If you'd enjoy making your own shampoo, try the Pioneer Web site at: http://www.pioneerthinking.com/shampoo2.html. Their basic recipe is for making shampoo from soapwart (saponaria officinalis). According to the Web site, "This contains saponins which is similar to soap. It lathers when agitated." Their site also includes ingredients such as catnip "to promote healthy hair growth" or Lemon Verbena for a citrus fragrance."

My own recipe for shampoo is simple. I mix 4 ounces of glycerine with a tablespoon of olive oil. Then I add ¼ cup of white distilled vinegar. I mix this into a quart of warm water into which three teabags of chamomile tea had been seeping for an hour, and stir. Then I add ¼ cup of Dove dishwashing liquid. I mix thoroughly and use this as shampoo. When I wash it out with water, I also put on a hair conditioner for two minutes and then wash it out with plain water.

I like washing my hair with tea—green tea (decaffeinated), chamomile tea, or rose hip tea, diluted with two quarts of water. After I lather my hair with any type of soapy mixture and rinse it out, I rinse the tea through my hair, and then apply hair conditioner, and finally rinse off the conditioner with more tea. Personally, I always add a small amount of olive oil to all my shampoos and home-made soaps.

Look at the Dollar Stretcher Web site at: http://www.stretcher.com/stories/981207b.cfm. It offers quite a number of homemade recipes for toiletries, shampoos, deodorants, and more. My own recipe for deodorant is to mix a paste of baking soda and water and mix with a little petroleum jelly or glycerin. Use as a salve. For toothpaste, I mix baking soda and water into a paste and use, then rinse with peroxide and finally water and mouthwash. Other sites include Herbal Gardens at: http://www.herbal-gardens.net/herbal-shampoo.htm for making your own shampoo. HealthRecipes.com has homemade beauty recipes at: http://www.healthrecipes.com/homemade_beauty_recipes.htm.

The Homemade Beauty Recipes site recommends a once-a-week honey mask on your face. According to the site, "Place a cloth in warm water and apply to your face to open the pores. Smear on honey, and leave on for 15 to 30 minutes. Rinse off with warm water. Then use cold water to close the pores."

Foods and cooking ingredients throughout history have been used as shampoos, deodorants, and toiletries. One of the oldest is olive oil. When you have made products from these types of ingredients and customized them for your needs, consider offering your customized products to others. If you can't actually make the product, offer your original recipes that you've tested and checked out with your health care professional for safety.

Dandruff-Treatment Shampoo

The Homemade Shampoo Web site at http://www.indianchild.com/homemade_shampoo.htm offers a recipe by L. Batra useful to treat dandruff. The site's recipe recommends 2 teaspoons dried rosemary, 2 teaspoons dried thyme, 2/3 cup boiling water, and 2/3 cup cider vinegar. According to L. Batra's recipe, you'll need to assemble a heatproof ceramic bowl, a fine sieve, and a clean 10 ounce plastic bottle with tightly fitting cover.

When you add boiling water to the herbs in the ceramic bowl, you cover and let the mixture steep for about 20 minutes. Then you strain out the herbs and add the 2/3 cups of cider vinegar to the water. You close the bottle and store in a cool, dry place. The Web site recipe recommends that you shampoo and rinse your hair. Then you massage a little of the herbal mixture into your scalp.

You can also massage a small amount between shampoos. The Web site recipe also notes that you can massage a small amount before going to bed. What's excellent about this herbal home-made dandruff treatment is that the herbs and vinegar create an environment that helps get rid of the bacteria and fungus that grow on those dead cells and bits of skin.

My own formula for getting rid of dandruff is to use cinnamon, cloves, chamomile, and honey massaged into the scalp and left on for a half hour. Then you rinse it off. You then put on your scalp a 'mask' of oatmeal and water—on short hair only. Let it stay another half hour, and rinse. Finally, shampoo as you usually do. Then apply your regular hair conditioner.

I make my own hair conditioner from ¼ cup of olive oil mixed with ¼ cup of rosemary essential oil. I mix the two oils and place in a tightly covered plastic bottle in the refrigerator. When I want the conditioner, I warm the oil in a pan of hot water, test it on my wrist so that it's body temperature, and then rub a tiny amount of the oil in my hair. I wrap a damp, steamy towel around my hair for an hour. Then I shampoo as usual to get the excess oil out.

Recipes for homemade hair conditioners are at the following Web sites: Somerset Cosmetic Company at: http://www.makingcosmetics.com/homemade-cosmetics-soaps/b02-formulation-hair-conditioner.htm, Pioneer Thinking (Rosemary hair conditioner) at: http://www.pioneerthinking.com/conditioner3.html using smaller amounts of oils than in my recipe, and at Care2 site at: http://www.care2.com/channels/solutions/self/1914 is an excellent homemade *mousse* formula for hair. It consists of beating two egg whites until it holds up in stiff peaks. Then you rub the egg whites into your hair, dry, and style. I tried this and didn't want to deal with the dried egg white meringue on my hair that attracted my two dogs, and they licked at my hair. However, it's up on the Web site as a homemade mousse recipe for hair. Some people like the beaten egg whites in their hair. My preference for a mousse is to have a slight fragrance of lemon or orange blossoms in my hair.

The Hair Care Recipes Cookbook is at: http://www.longlocks.com/hair-care-recipes-cookbook.htm. This is an excellent Web site. For example, their hair conditioner recipe calls for mayonnaise and avocado—a small jar of mayonnaise and one avocado. Another recipe calls for coconut milk and avocado blended. You work the mixture through your hair for 15 minutes and rinse. Other conditioners at the site use jojoba oil mixed with soybean oil.

They also have a rosemary hair conditioning recipe using dried rosemary leaves mixed with soybean oil. This Web site's treatment for dandruff consists of ginger root, sesame oil, and lemon juice. You juice the ginger root through a sieve and use a tablespoon of ginger juice mixed with a teaspoon of sesame oil and a teaspoon of lemon juice. The site also has an excellent hair conditioner made from a cup of warm beer mixed with a teaspoon of jojoba oil.

Basically, you can use any oil suitable for the scalp. My favorite is olive oil. You can mix the oil with any liquid that is kind to your skin. When you leave the oil mixture on for 15-45 minutes under a hot, steamy towel, and then shampoo out, your hair basically feels softer and cleaner. In ancient times people used to use olive oil instead of soap. They scraped off the oil with dead skin. Then they washed with water and a variety of herbs and scents.

The Web site does have a chamomile brightener for blonde hair. You take chamomile tea and add ½ cup plain yogurt and a little lavender oil. Then you cover your head in a plastic wrap and let it condition for a half hour before shampooing with your normal shampoo.

All the Web sites I checked out recommend a variety of herbs, oils, and foods such as yogurt to condition hair. Research them all for yourself and decide which works best for you. Better yet, develop your own original formula. Mine is to wash my hair with glycerin, mild dish soap, and apple cider vinegar in small amounts. Then I condition with olive oil and orange blossom extract (water). Then I shampoo with chamomile tea. My favorite scent for my hair rinse water is vanilla and water.

Interestingly, the LongLocks Hair Care Web site at: <u>http://www.longlocks.</u> <u>com/hair-care-recipes-cookbook.htm</u> also has a red hair enhancer made from ½ cup each of beet juice mixed with carrot juice. You put it on your hair, sit in the sun or under a dryer or warm towel for an hour, and then shampoo out. This is for people with natural red or auburn hair. Don't try it on snow-white hair. Their natural color restorer for **_gray hair_** calls for 2 cups of dried sage and 1/4 cup dried rosemary.

You simmer two cups of water with the rosemary and sage for 30 minutes. Let the mixture stand for a few hours. Then you applied the mixture to gray hair and allow it to dry. You finally shampoo.

Each week the recipe asks you to repeat the process until your hair reaches the color you want. Then you do the process again each month. I haven't tried it yet on my snow-white hair. I'd like it back to medium ash blonde using natural herbs. This is my favorite project to search—for an herbal hair tint that doesn't make any changes inside the body.

37

Shoes

How do you craft and sew custom-made-to-fit shoes from scratch? To get an idea of how to make your own shoes for comfort and tailored fit, first explore online instructions for making your own shoes. Keep in mind that if you have growing children or grand children, making custom-made shoes is a wonderful gift, and it does cut expenses and at the same offer comfort and benefits.

Making your family's shoes is another way to live on less while having more. It enhances your creativity and thinking skills. The shoes can be of better quality. And it fits under the label of household necessities to enjoy within the basic food, shelter, and clothing category.

Put your own designer label on your home-made shoes and offer to design custom-fit shoes for others. That's one more way to make money at home or online with your creativity. You can make shoes for yourself and your family or for others. Crafting, sewing, and practical creativity give you more choices when you're aiming to cut expenses and enjoy more comfort.

Start with the Web sites and books on how to make your own shoes. Excellent Web sites include Make Your Own Shoes, a step-by-step guide for high fashion, low-cost, and perfect fit. The Web site features illustrated instructions for making shoes from scratch. Every step is illustrated. The site is at: http://www.marywalesloomis.com/page3.html.

What I like about these instructions is that the author, Mary Wales Loomis, also has written a book on how to make your own shoes. The details are at: http://www.marywalesloomis.com/page10.html. In addition to her book, which you can order, her Web site gives instructions on how to make shoes.

The instructions show how you use your existing shoes to make a last by reshaping plaster of Paris to change width or toe shape on the last. Included are detailed instructions for casting your feet to make a custom-made last from which you can make different types of shoes to match your clothing or accessories. At the site: http://www.marywalesloomis.com/page4.html illustrations include a list of the materials you will need and instructions on how to make a muslin pattern and sew the shoe. The illustrations show the materials you'll need in forming the uppers to join the lasts.

You learn with illustrations and explanations how to sew the back seam and put the uppers onto the lasts. For example, you wet the upper and form it onto the last so it can dry in the shape of the last. This is illustrated at the site. The instructions are excellent, especially in recommending strong thread so the upper can be sewn tightly to the last and left to dry.

The site shows you how to apply a certain type of cement to the heels and attach the sole. For those who aren't able to access the Web or use computers, the book is full of excellent illustrated instructions on how to make your own shoes. You can make them at far less cost than you'd ever buy custom-made shoes that fit perfectly. You have the power to control what materials you want to use for your shoes. The benefit is you get to make shoes for yourself or anyone else that match other clothing or accessories. There are several other sites on the Web on making your own shoes.

What you need to do before you make anything such as shoes is to take a shoe apart or anything else apart to make a pattern and to see how they are made. It's a type of back-engineering with basic clothing that mystifies a lot of us.

You start by putting in front of you two comfortable pairs of shoes that will be 'sacrificed.' Begin by assembling a hammer, screwdriver, and pliers. Then take apart an old shoe that was very comfortable and broken-in to the shape of your foot.

Now take another complete pair of shoes that have not been taken apart. Use your most comfortable shoes that have seen their day, but are stretched and molded to fit your foot. The key word is comfortable. Use the most comfortable pair of shoes you have.

You're going to make a mold by filling your most comfortable pair of shoes with plaster of Paris. When the plaster dries, you carefully cut the shoe away from the plaster, saving the tops of the shoes for your pattern. Now you have your mold. This mold is called a set of 'lasts.' Save those tops to make a pattern out of muslin fabric.

You'll use fabric that matches your other clothing or accessories for the outside of the shoe. Buckram is used to shape the inside of the shoe and give it some support for your foot.

When you sew it all together, you will be putting water on the upper part of the shoe to form it onto the plaster lasts. Then you let it dry on the last so that it makes a custom fit in the shape of your old comfortable shoe.

You'll need finer details of what type of shoe to make. Some books show you how to make a ladies' pump. So for making shoes for men or boys, you'll need to use men's shoes. The best way to start is to buy a book on how to make shoes and learn the finer details of materials to use.

You'll need to learn how to change the plaster of Paris mold of your foot into the shape of a shoe. The crude type of shape from your shoe is different from the exact plaster of Paris cast of your foot that you'll need to customize the shoe to fit comfortably on your foot. That's why it's best to start by reading a book on how to use the plaster of Paris cast of your foot and how to change it into the shape of a shoe.

Mary's book illustrates how to make the soles of your shoes by hand-cutting them from tooling leather. She also lists resources to buy the leather. There's a chapter on making flat shoes. Some people don't wear leather shoes. So you choose what materials you want. To order Mary's book, see her Web site at: http://www.marywalesloomis.com/page10.html.

There are other Web sites on how to make your own shoes. For example, learn to make your own shoes at the Web site at: http://www.inquiry.net/outdoor/ winter/gear/snowshoes/. The site gives instructions for making "Indian" snow-shoes made from wood, pioneer snowshoes from ash or hickory sticks, Alaskan shoes (includes patterns and plans), Chippewa snowshoes with pointers on varia-tions including bear paw, co-Yukon, Sioux, Oregon, Utah, Montreal, and Iro-quois snowshoes. There also are instructions on making snowshoe bindings for use with snowshoe moccasins, and bindings made for boots.

38

Toys

Grand River Toys at: http://www.grandrivertoys.com/pages/MakeYourOwn.html offers kits on making your own toys. One example is the kit for making your own ice cream. There's another kit for making your own chocolate. Kits include making your own comic book, talking clock, bubble gum, jigsaw puzzle, a volcano-making kit, a milk carton radio, a tooth fairy treasure chest, a sensory dome, and lots of other kits for making toys, digital recording labs, crystal wonders, pinhole cameras, and food items.

The easiest way to make a toy is to take one apart and back-engineer it to see how it fits together, piece by piece. Old-fashioned toys made of wood or fabric or toys focused on making CDs have different methods of construction. Toys, fabric, and pillows can easily be turned turn into soft pet beds.

The Web site, Physics Toys at: http://fog.ccsf.cc.ca.us/~tbardin/ has a section on how to make your own toys that explain physics. It's at: http://fog.ccsf.cc.ca.us/~tbardin/html/toys.html. Check out this site to learn how to make toys illustrating the principles of electrostatics, magnetism electromagnetism, buoyancy, fluid pressures, fluid dynamics, heat energy, evaporation, phase changes, forces, motion, momentum, energy, light waves, image formations, sound waves, standing waves and wave motions. How about making a toy the whole family can enjoy and continuously contribute to?

What kind of toys or board games can you make from item you have around the house? Games from cardboard boxes, craft items, and knitted toys such as teddy bears all can be made from existing objects such as pillows and sweaters. It enhances your creativity to think of new items to make out of what you already have or could easily and inexpensively obtain. The whole idea is to have fun, and increase benefits, comfort, health, quality, and custom-fit while decreases expenses. You also want to be good to the environment and exercise your brain and body. It's the redemptive value that's your motivation for making it yourself from scratch.

Open an Online 'Toybrary'

Look at the success of a popular videotape game called <u>Clue</u>, from Parker Brothers. As soon as the tape was released, it immediately sold more than 100,000 units. By the mid-eighties, Park Brothers sold more than 300,000, about 90 percent marketed to toy stores.

Today, the trend moves from camcorder to DVD to computer. Visual anthropology and sociology, current issues, and life stories move from camcorder to DVD in one take. Life stories feed into computer hard disks to be downloaded by anyone anywhere with fast broadband and saved on a disk. Education and toys mix so that learning can be fun again.

Earn money with your video camcorder by producing, editing, distributing, or selling your videos to toy stores. You can create a video toy library: a toybrary, where children can rent video games as if they were toys donated to a library.

Sell or rent children's videos by mail order, out of your home, or in your own video thrift store—operating like an old time radio tape rental library. If your video focuses on activities children enjoy, or can be viewed by families, try the toy store market for your video game or video storytelling. Create videos to be used as toys.

INCOME POTENTIAL:

If you sell your video game at low prices, or have a low-priced (under $30) videocassette, it might interest toy stores. The toy market recently represented more than $10 billion in sales.

If you can price your video really low, it might interest the more than 375 super toy stores in the United States and the more than 1,200 toy specialty outlets. Children's video sales are big business. A growing market exists in interactive children's videos also.

Price your videos for children under $30, and contact the children's video libraries. The video genre of children's programming is the fastest and largest growing market of non-movie videos carried by both toy stores and video stores.

You can also sell to the publishing market. Well known children's book publishers have entered the video business. Like them, you, too can produce, acquire, or distribute children's videos.

Children's bookstores usually prefer videos priced under $15. Many bookstores carry children's videos priced as cheaply as $9 or less. The cheaper you can price your videos, the more stores will be interested in taking them in to sell.

BEST LOCALE TO OPERATE THE BUSINESS:

Try the toy stores first. Bookstores that carry videos really want outstanding video hits. However, there is an expanding market for children's educational videos, teen magazine videos, calendars, information, health, children's animation, and music videos. Books on video are popular, particularly favorite children's books that can be brought to life on tape and marketed to toy chains.

Here's a list of the most interested businesses to buy books to put on video: mystery, suspense, romance, mainstream, historical romance, adventure, science fiction, western, humor/comedy, supernatural, scientific toy research, and war/military. If your video is nonfiction storytelling for kids, the favorite genres are instruction, reference, biography, religious, health, exercise, and for adults, home repair, gardening, how-to, craft, leisure/travel, investments, and last—doing your tax paperwork.

If you try to get your videos in bookstores, be aware that bookstores expect a 45 percent margin or higher. Orders take quite a while to fill. As a video-maker, the bookstore long margins may bother you.

New video titles are announced two months before release. So orders are demanded long before the video is available. This does not agree with bookstores who order only quarterly. If you're dealing with mass market merchandisers, they also order only quarterly.

Since video has carved a permanent niche in bookstores, the two fields—publishing and video-making have a lot to learn from one another to make production go smoother. The outlook is that whatever is a hit in book form could soon become a videocassette meant for home viewing by the family.

In the industry, children's video represents more than a $50 million wholesale business for toy stores, including educational tapes sold by toy stores. Video tapes are even sold in the children's department of many stores. Some new video makers are putting greeting card videos for children on tape.

If the average parent spends more than $170 a year on toys for each child, about 50 percent are impulse items. Toy stores like to push videocassettes displayed as customers walk in or as they wait to pay the cashier—as one of their favorite impulse items.

If you want to begin as a video vendor before you make your own videos, try the toy stores first—before the book stores. Video retailers put their orders in for new cassettes every 30 days. When the toy stores finally orders, they want big profit margins and high return agreements. People who make videos don't like giving these lee ways to the toy store owners. So, to make money, focus on giving a unique presentation or game on your video.

TRAINING REQUIRED:

To make a video for toy store sales, focus on children's or family programming. You don't need formal training, but learn what sells to children by reading the toy trade journals and joining the business trade associations.

GENERAL APTITUDE OR EXPERIENCE:

You should like to entertain children and know what's popular. Animation, games, storytelling, or putting your writings on video, if they are popular with children helps. You can also try storytelling for an adult audience or a video game the whole family can play.

If you invent a new kind of video bingo-type game, or use your original cartoon character, training in animation design helps. You can get such training or hire an animation artist by consulting "animators" in your local Yellow Pages directory.

VIDEO EQUIPMENT NEEDED:

You'll need a video camera, editing equipment, and good story material, animation, and special effects. The quickest way to obtain animation on tape is to ask a student in animation or a hungry new animator to design from your story script and go 50-50 on any profits made from sales. Copyright your work. For animation, a computer is necessary with animation software. You'll need equipment that interfaces your video camera, VCR, and personal computer, and any other special effects and animation software.

The cheapest route is to approach any community college that has a major in animation and ask for students to help you or to intern with you in exchange for college credits, or to hire a new animator who needs experience and a tape to use as a portfolio piece.

OPERATING YOUR BUSINESS:

Begin to design your game or tell your story on video with either live actors using your material in script or play form, or if a game, computer animation and voice-over simulations. If you're going interactive, you'll need a freelance crew of programmers, technicians, artists, writers, and yourself as producer-packager to deal with distributors and toy stores.

To get specific instruction, step-by-step in creating original video games, network with members of video and computer game designers' professional associations and inquire of animation students how they get their ideas. That will inspire and motivate you to invent your own video game. Everyone's is original and unique, yet appeals to popular tastes in video games. So study the video game market thoroughly.

One great annual conference of video, computer, and interactive game designers is the TED Conferences, Inc., The Orchard, 180 Narragansett Ave., Newport Rhode Island 02840.

To make money putting your storytelling on video, you can round up actors, readers, writers, and professional storytellers and create a unique character such as a foster grandparent who reads children's stories on video for special occasions—birthday party entertainment, bedtime stories for preschoolers, or any unique audience you want to target with your stories on video.

Add the spice of special effects and animation combined with live actors and readers, and you have a great storytelling experience on video. You can begin by showing your video at professional storyteller's associations, and then market to retailers, bookstores, record stores, video chains, toy stores, and the rental market.

Find out whether your storytelling videos or your video game cassettes would be better suited to the sell-through market or the rental market. These two separate markets for video product have different prices and different material.

Videos that are rented by consumers are geared for quick turnover. The videos go to stores at higher prices than the cheaper videos meant for sale.

Most movies are high-priced videos going to rental markets. Most toy-store videos are cheap videos or video games meant to sell to parents and children.

Don't price your video, toy, or board game higher than the average cost of books, records, audio tapes, and music compact disks. Your video can sell in convenience stores, through mass merchants, at sports stores if it has to do with athletics, exercise, or health, through direct mail, or through direct response television infomercials.

You'll have to package your video or toy to attract attention. Advertising and pricing will determine whether your video will become popular. Nobody can look at a DVD in a toy store, unlike books that can be read in the store. *Packaging* sells your video, board game, or toy, not 'browsability'.

If you go in for storytelling and video games, you'll be competing in the children's market and in toystores, competing against Disney, Family Home Entertainment, Kids Klassics, Scholastic, and all the big names in book publishing and home video production, like Vestron, Sony, and Western Publishing. You'll also be competing against the interactive multimedia computer game market that uses video interactively with computer animation and story telling—music, lights, text, and art.

Keep your tape for children under one hour in length. Price it under $20. Storytelling works best around a theme, especially a holiday theme. If you aren't doing animation themes, focus on a holiday celebration or animal themes.

You can also do an exercise for children's tape, focusing on preschoolers, or present on video your own children's books, featuring live actors. One excellent example is the Beatrice Potter stories on video. Classic characters from children's story books, if you can get the rights or write great stories, make classic children's video.

TARGET MARKET:

You want your video games or storytelling on tape to reach toy stores and bookstores. You can also market through direct mail order to clients whose names already appear on lists which you can buy—people who have bought videos my mail order before.

Storytelling video markets include schools and parents, bookstores, and writer's circles.

RELATED VIDEO OPPORTUNITIES:

Besides video games or storytelling videos, you can work with animators to create unique characters to fit special occasions, such as children's birthday parties. Or you can use videos to present themes to schools, such as tapes on self-esteem for children, cultural diversity, or psychological themes, such as why some children need to be the center of attention, others need approval, and others need to be the class clown. Another theme is dealing with difficult people such as the school bully or finding ways to deal with learning disabilities and discovering aptitudes or enhancing creativity.

Social studies and controversial themes also make good videos. A related opportunity is to acquire pamphlets on hot issues in the news or controversy and create videos for the junior high school social studies classes. Entertainment and learning are often combined on popular-selling videos.

ADDITIONAL INFORMATION:

Vidion/International Association of Video
1440 N. St. NW, Ste. 601
Washington, DC 20005
(202) 328-9346

Video Software Dealers Association
303 Harper Dr.
Morristown, NJ 08057-3229
(609) 231-7800

Cyber Society
C/O Greg Klein
2016 Main St., Ste. 1207
Houston, TX 77002-8843
(713) 752-0761
(Clearing house for virtual reality products and technology.)

Home Video Publisher
Knowledge Industry Publications
701 Westchester Ave.
White Plains, NY 10604

Listening Library Inc.
One Park Ave.
Old Greenwich, CT 06870
(203) 637-3616

American Video Network
830 S. Myrtle Rd.
Monrovia, CA 91016
1(800) 523-5193 (Wholesaler/Distributor)

Association of Visual Communicators
8130 La Mesa Blvd.
#406
La Mesa, CA 91941-6437
(619) 461-1600

University Consortium for Instructional Development and Technology
c/o Dr. Kent L. Gustafson
Dept. of Instructional Technology
607 Aderhold Hall, University of Georgia

Athens, GA 30602
(706) 542-3810

Commission on Instructional Technology
C/O Superintendent of Documents
US Government Printing Office
Washington, DC 20402
(202) 275-2051

39

Travel and Free Walking Tours

Two types of free tours exist if you're looking for free travel. The first kind is where you visit a city and take advantage of the free tours offered of the city. These usually are walking tours of streets, galleries, government buildings, theaters, or museums on free admission day. Make a list of cities and check the Web at sites such as Chicago Traveler at: http://www.chicagotraveler.com/attractions/chicago-greeter-free-tours.html, or New York City for Visitors at: http://gonyc.about.com/cs/toursbr/a/bigapplegreeter.htm, or The Paramount (free theater tour) at: http://www.theparamount.com/artists/public-tour.asp. When you use your search engine with the key words "free tours," you'll see a list of cities or places that offer free guided walking tours of an area or buildings.

When you visit a city and don't know anyone, don't have a car, don't know the bus, trolley, or train schedule, and don't know where to go, a free tour can help you to meet new people, walk in safety with a group, and learn some historic or contemporary information about a particular area. In New York City, for example, check out the free walking tours by viewing the Web site at: http://www.newyorkmetro.com/urban/guides/nyonthecheap/pleasures/walkingtours.htm.

The advantage of a free walking tour is that you learn details that people who lived there may never have heard. The New York metro.com site contains a headline from an article that explains: "Free walking tours dish the dirt on neighborhoods, landmarks, parks, and celebrities. Rediscover City classics or set out for the road less traveled."

Check out the San Francisco City Guides site at: http://www.sfcityguides.org/ where free walking tours of San Francisco have been offered for the past 25 or more years. If you really love any city, its history, lore and legends, you can volunteer to offer free walking tours. Build experience by volunteering in your area. When you've learned the lore of any city you want to travel too, consider gathering a group of tourists or travelers who will pay to travel with you to a particular city. You go to that part of the world free in exchange for conducting a walking tour of that city.

There are in many cities, people who give walking tours for pay. They usually negotiate with a tour bus or travel service to give a number of tours in an agreed upon time frame for commission or pay.

You can offer walking tours free as a volunteer, or organize a walking tour business of your own. To get paid and still go free on the tour, you'd have to get a certain number of people to pay for the tour and work out a deal with the airlines, cruise ship, hotel, hostel, school, tour bus or travel service whereby you work by giving a certain number of tours in exchange for free travel.

Another way to go free is to run your business from scratch. Tourists pay you a fee. You make all the arrangements, and take them on a walking tour of a certain country or city. Your fee per person would be enough to pay for your lodging and travel expenses.

After you've taken several free walking tours of any city, consider whether you'd like to start a home-based business offering walking tours of any city, anywhere in the world that you'd like to see and where walking tours are relatively safe.

Find out what kind of insurance you need and which travel agencies you want to contact. Promote your walking tours in travel and entertainment publications and Web sites that reach tourists and travelers, including business travelers and those attending conventions.

You could conduct walking tours of any city, anywhere. Often travel agencies have arrangements. Some stipulate that if you find a certain number of paying tourists to go take a tour of a particular area that you can come along free as the tour guide.

Or start your own independent walking tour that specializes in taking people to another part of the world. If you sign up enough paying tourists, you can go free, if those type of arrangements are made with your travel agent, a particular cruise company, hotel, hostel, or as part of your own independent business.

WALKING AS A BUSINESS

If you love to walk, contact various offices of any type where the people usually sit all day. Offer to take groups on lunch hour walks in a particular area of the city in which you live. Take the office employees—whether you work there or not—on long walks during the flexible lunch hour.

Start a home-based weekend-only neighborhood walking tour business on a shoestring budget. Give your walking tour business a name such as "Inside Details" or "Images and History." Pick an original name for your business that explains in two words what you offer on your walking tour. Start with sedentary office workers and offer lunchtime walks with a stop so they can sit somewhere and eat or buy lunch, sit down, and eat for 15 minutes before walking back to the office as a group.

During vacation periods from your usual weekday job, take tourists on walking tours all over the most fascinating cities of different countries. Pick a country that's relatively safe for walking. Eventually, your walking tour business can offer international walking tours of foreign cities as well as local, neighborhood, and wilderness sites.

You start local at first, obtain knowledge of where to walk in which countries or cities, and finally, turn your small business, into an international walking business with a new name that explains where you walk. Finally, turn your international walking business into a nonprofit group dedicated to promoting neighborhood walking in urban, suburban, and rural environments throughout the world. As you expand, you'll have to hire people to run the walking tours seven days a week. You also can work with volunteers as well as paid employees. You decide how far you want to go as a nonprofit group with a commitment to promoting safe walking around the world.

You can charge a small fee, such as $3 or walking, or let everyone walk free and operate as a nonprofit business to promote safe walking for health and stress reduction. You can cater to older adults or office workers or all age groups, or specialize in walking for people with special needs.

If you operate as a nonprofit agency, you can offer free walking tours and run on donations to your nonprofit agency. You'll be able to maintain a rented office with a volunteer staff if enough donations come in for your nonprofit safe walking tour group.

Most people would not like to spend a fee for walking. You'll probably find your people dropping because the walks cover the same area repeatedly. So it's best to operate as a nonprofit agency and run on donations with a volunteer staff rather than a paid staff.

To bring in more money, publish a newsletter listing walking times for an annual $10 or $12 subscription. When running your non-profit walking tour service, make a list of categories to which people can contribute money. Out-of-town trips will generate more income. In addition, the volunteer walking leaders can arrange their own trips and go through your nonprofit safe walking tour service to take walkers on tours of foreign cities or national locations if they can find enough walkers willing to walk through the cities selected at an agreed-upon price. They have to work up a budget.

For the working crowds, keep offering midweek lunch break walks. Some of these office workers will be happy to take your walking tours to other countries when they get vacation time. Your clients would be sedentary office workers.

Other features offered by your free and safe walking tours in addition to offering walking the various neighborhoods of your area could include a once-a week lunch group that visits different ethnic restaurants. You can offer a Saturday walk for older adults or singles so they can walk and chat.

Offer free walks through local parks focusing on older adults or singles groups to meet, walk, and talk. One day of the week offer a walk through various wilderness sites in your area. Schedule different types of walks throughout the week depending upon demand and needs of various age groups and special interest groups.

Besides walking within one city, take a group for a weekend trip to another nearby city to see a show and spend two days overnight for a reasonable price—perhaps for under $200. Contact a reputable bus line and take your group to mountain resorts or other areas where they can walk safely. Make sure you and everyone else has insurance in case something happens to someone on a walk. Keep insured for surprises.

Take walkers to see a play or other event combined with a day of walking. Let them see a show and rest after a walk, and make sure there are places for them to eat, perhaps at different ethnic restaurants or have a take out lunch. Take the walkers to a resort where they can have a wine and cheese party and in the summer, use of a swimming pool (provided the resort, you, and the walkers are insured against accidents or other surprises). Make sure you have liability insurance.

Your walkers would enjoy a Sunday spent with breakfast at a hotel followed by a tram ride and a sightseeing walk. Let them look at lakes. Keep rules, such as never allowing a tourist to pass the leader. If they walk ahead of the leader, don't let them participate again in the walk. You need to follow these rules for safety. No one can walk ahead of the leader or move out of site. You don't want people getting lost in a mountain or wilderness setting or moving out of site and being late or missing for the ride home.

To start your walking regimen, lead a downtown walking group. Specialize in older adults or the group you want. Morning walks starting at about 10 or 11

AM are excellent for older adults. Take your walkers on a golf course walk around dinner time—between 5 and 6 PM.

Another walking group can start with a train ride to the old town of your city followed by an hour and a half walk with a stop for a refreshing snack and water, including breaks for restroom use. Older adults and non-drivers who use public transportation usually prefer morning, afternoon, or early evening walks.

For all ages, Saturday night walks are excellent as free entertainment. In addition, Saturday night walks traditionally draw younger singles and those who still drive. Families with young children in strollers enjoy morning or afternoon walks on weekends.

You also can offer an early Saturday morning hike if you live near a mountain. Volunteers can take this tour with walkers in good condition who like steep and strenuous walks. For persons who need to take it easy, Saturdays could unfold at 8:30 AM, beginning with eating together at the Y or elsewhere, meeting people, and chatting, followed by a volunteer-led mild walking tour of downtown or another area that offers historic and cultural points of interest.

As a nonprofit service, your walks can continue all day with a variety of volunteers focusing on different areas such as a river walk, a beachcomber walk. At 6:00 PM, you could have a volunteer conduct an evening walk. Offer a Sunday breakfast walk at 7:00 or 9:00 AM, followed by a merry-go-round walk at 8:00 AM. By 3:30 PM, you could offer a coffee or high tea walk led by volunteers. Different volunteers would offer the walking tours each day of the week.

Your high tea walk could offer herbal tea followed by walks past your harbor or other point of interest to enjoy sights and sounds. In winter, volunteers could show the walkers the colorful sunset on a 5:00 pm. Spend Sunday evenings at a coffee or tea house for an optional visit after the walk. Offer flat walks for those who can't climb steep sidewalks or hills. Classify your walks into mild and moderate. Offer a large variety of walks and give your walking group a name.

Find fit volunteers to offer family fitness walks at 9:00 AM one day a week when families can walk together. At 10:45, a good time for older adults who don't like getting up early in the morning for 7:00 or 9:00 am walks, offer a mild walk. Award a price for the oldest walker.

Take senior citizens from various senior community centers on a mild one-hour stroll that emphasizes spectacular views, including views from high-rise buildings from the inside as well as outdoors. For example, many seniors like to look at views from the 40th floor or higher of a building to see the panorama of their city. Others like to stroll outdoors. Include wheelchair walks for those who use power chairs and scooters as well. Walk at the pace of the slowest walker and have volunteers trained to work with older adults. Patience is a virtue when people need to walk slowly. The goal is enjoyment of the walk, stress reduction, and relaxation.

Take walkers on tours of high-priced homes or home tours when available. Looking at the outside of expensive homes is free, whereas looking inside a home, usually around the holidays, usually costs money that often is donated to charities to raise funds for various causes. Morning tours are best for viewing expensive homes from the street. Make sure the homes don't have loose dogs running in the street before you take a group on a walk of neighborhood sidewalks.

Your nonprofit walking service needs several vice presidents, a treasurer, secretary, and numerous corresponding secretaries. Have an emphasis for your nonprofit group dedicated to walking—such as family fitness. Make sure special groups are taken on walks, such as those with disabilities. To contribute to causes, do fundraising as a nonprofit group.

Make sure any leaders are trained and certified where fitness is concerned. Conduct several walks as fundraisers. Shoes are important in the walking business. Contact shoe manufacturers. Negotiate with companies that sell walking shoes to help you arrange a shoe fund and annual picnic. Ask the manufacturers and sellers of walking shoes to provide shoes to needy children in your area. Support your shoe fund.

You'll find that there will be some people who like to walk for miles. Others want to stroll around posh areas. Volunteers who are trained, certified, and fit can conduct walks for those who are fit enough to take eight-mile hikes. Schedule the walks around the lovely areas of your town. Include the expensive and beautiful country clubs, the places famous for attracting vacationing movie stars, and resorts or hotels with golf courses that attract the wealthy and world-class golf professionals.

What you need for your nonprofit walking group are high teas and coffee klatches. The best day for these events is on each Fridays morning after the walk or at noon lunches after the walk. It's one of the "Thank God It's Friday" type of events. After a Friday morning walk or at lunch time after the noontime walk, a lot of office workers still have spare time to get back to the office. So make time for lunch. Or offer your high tea at 9:45 instead of the usual 4:00 PM.

Walkers will look forward to stops for scrumptious breakfasts are made after the early morning walks that might typically run from 7:45 to 9:45. Friday morning walks followed by breakfast or lunch are for those with flexible working hours and retirees. Early morning, lunch, and after-work hours draw a crowd of office workers, work-at-home parents, people who work afternoon shifts, and those into family fitness.

Total family fitness walks can be your most popular offering. Schedule at 9:00 AM a toddlers and grandparents walk together around flat areas such as lakes or beach areas that run about a mile in length. Allow families to decide how many laps around a lake, beach, park, or other area they want to walk. They can choose a nature trail or the sidewalk to finish the workout.

Include training and walking, a jaunt with lunch, or a midweek wilderness walk on trails plus lunch. Train and certify your volunteers on how to lead people on walks. Give them awards.

Talk to newspaper reporters about your need to recruit volunteers to lead the walks with free training provided. The training is not only about safe walking. It's also about the sights and events discussed on the walks. Leaders can earn money by taking walkers on their own customized walking tours anywhere.

On one of your walks, include seeing a musical play. For example, an hour's walk can complement taking in a dramatic theater play at a discounted fee. The walkers could meet in front of the theater at matinee or evening time, walk for an hour, and return at 1:45 PM or 6:45 PM to wait for the play performance in the theater.

Focus on walking throughout the world as a fitness recreation. Classify your walkers and volunteer leaders as casual, moderate, moderate/plus, brisk, and very brisk, depending upon the speed at which the group walks. Casual is clocked at 2-3 miles per hour, moderate, 3 miles per hour, moderate/plus, 3 ½ miles per hour, brisk, 4 miles per hour, and very brisk, more than 4 miles per hour.

Start a nonprofit walking group that attracts a certain group of people—for example, families with children, fitness enthusiasts, older adults and retirees, singles, sedentary office workers, persons with special needs, mall walkers, artists, photographers looking for a clearer focus, birdwatchers, dog-walkers, or a job/client-hunting community seeking to net-walk. Your photographers, artists, or birdwatchers may want to stroll with cameras, camcorders, or sketch pads ready for the unexpected in nature.

Don't forget the large number of people, including older adults who enjoy morning or noontime mall walking as exercise. If you want to learn how an actual nonprofit walking group operates, contact the National Organization of Mall Walkers, at PO Box 191, Hermann, MO 65041. Check out Web sites at: http://www.peternielsen.com/walking.htm and at: http://www.chiropractic-software.com/mall_walking.htm. If you want to bring more walkers to malls for walking combined with culture rather than shopping, offer poetry or drama readings in shopping malls, perhaps near food courts and book stores. Reading excerpts from books near a bookstore might also bring in the walkers, and the food courts may look inviting even to rest, after a long mall walk.

Design your own walking program. See the Web site at: http://www. peternielsen.com/walking.htm. For more information, *The Rockport Guide to Lifelong Fitness* tells you more about an easy-to-use test that helps you design your own walking program. Send a self-addressed, 45-cent stamped envelope to Walking Test, The Rockport Walking Institute, 220 Donald Lynch Blvd. PO Box 480, Marlboro, MA 01752.

40

Censored News

DESCRIPTION OF BUSINESS:

Cover the news that didn't make the news, exposing corporate, institutional, or government corruption through your investigative video reporting. Your video could carry the news that didn't make the newspapers because of censors.

Make a video of underground news. Be an investigative video reporter and expose corruption. Be a video muckraker and raise hell. To understand muckraking video, you need to know a little about what it's like in print.

Read Jessica Mitford's introduction to <u>Poison Penmanship: The Gentle Art of Muckraking</u>. Mitford's investigative writing led to social change by inspiring and motivating the public. In 1963, she exposed the funeral industry in her book, <u>The American Way of Death</u>. Beneficial changes resulted. Therefore, your video surely can find subjects to explore, muckrake, and expose.

INCOME POTENTIAL:

Since fewer than 20 corporations now control most of the United State's mass media, your income potential as an independent is unlimited as long as you cover the subject of information control and how it exploits our minds. Any video on mind manipulation is sure to earn an income for you depending on repetition.

To make a successful video, you must use continuous and lasting propaganda. You must not leave any gaps. If your video lasts a long time, you can expect to gross between $20 and $40 on each video.

Expensive videos usually sell through direct mail order for $39.95. Popular mail order DVDs are priced around $19.95 to $29.95. There are low-cost documentaries and DVD movies for sale online for less—for $5 or $7, plus shipping. You can offer a video mail order distributor a commission to sell your video at their own prices. Make sure that whatever you price your video at that you make a profit and at the same time the video is cheap enough to attract enough customers who think it's a fair price and affordable.

Do a test mailing first to find out your viewer's opinion of the price in relation to the content. Is it really affordable by the majority of your potential market?

The rule is the lower priced the tape, the more copies it will sell. Video stores will only take it if it's priced low enough to have high turnover, and if they can get their cut of your profit.

You could be better off with your own mail order flyer going to a list of club members interested in the subject of your video. If you charge anywhere from $19.95 to $30 to the public by direct mail order, you can expect some income from clubs, workshops, seminars, and association meetings, as well as video-of-the-month clubs. Sell your tapes at a discount during meetings and conventions.

Getting your video into stores usually means it would have to air first—either in front of a national convention of video software dealers, or on the local or public broadcast news—or run as a documentary on one of the news magazine shows on television or on cable television. Create visibility by airing your video at conventions of people interested in the subject matter of your tape.

The tape can make the national meeting rounds. Usually every month there's a convention or conference in different cities of local chapters of various associations, clubs, or organizations interested in the subject matter of your tape. Call public speakers who travel around the country giving presentations at conventions and ask them to show your tape during the meeting or pass flyers out to the captured convention audience.

BEST LOCALE TO OPERATE THE BUSINESS:

You can run your muckraking video production company from any location where there is censored news to be exposed to the public. It's not necessary to live in any special city, but you'll need to have rapport with the underground video and alternate media/broadcast industry as well as the standard media old boys network.

Being in Washington, DC will help if it's government or the military you plan to expose in your videos. It's better to be near the large broadcast media firms in New York, but you have to be on the road all over to tape your investigative reports.

TRAINING REQUIRED:

If you already know how to run your industrial quality camcorder, the next subject to learn is investigative reporting. You can get in touch with the Investigative Journalism Project (Fund for Constitutional Government), 122 Maryland Ave NE, Suite 300, Washington, DC 20002 (202) 546-3732, or join IRE (Investigative Reporters and Editors), 100 Neff Hall, University of Missouri, School of Journalism, Columbia, MO 65211. This organization puts out enough publications to train you at home to be a great investigative reporter if only from reading what they publish—journals, newsletters, books, etc.

Or contact Media Watch, Media Alliance, or the Media Institute (addresses are in the appendices at the back of this book). There are enough publications published by the media organizations (listed in the back of this book) to help make you an investigative reporter using video as your medium of expression. You also can connect to the Internet on your personal computer and exchange information with people all over the country and abroad.

GENERAL APTITUDE OR EXPERIENCE:

Good interviewing skills are essential. You need to be a bit of a private investigator, have a willingness to expose corruption, and have an interest in finding out what's happening that affects most people's lives in a universal way. A journalism writing aptitude helps, or a partner who does the writing while you do the technical video work.

Muckraking videos really do dig up the dirt and expose it to the public in order to have beneficial changes made. Generally, you should really want to save the world in a small way with your video camera and have a nose for news.

VIDEO EQUIPMENT NEEDED:

You'll need your broadcast quality field camera, tape, batteries, sound, lighting, and editing equipment, mobility, and a readiness to travel anywhere to videotape the news or expose corruption. Some taping will be in the homes of people you'll be interviewing.

OPERATING YOUR BUSINESS:

Making underground videos out of news that usually is censored each year has to be one of the most exciting ways to earn money with your video camera. To begin, first you spot important, but overlooked news in the back pages of your local newspaper—or the newspaper in some small town.

Perhaps it's news of ecological disaster. Or you want to make a video on why 12 million children go hungry in this country each day because you saw an alarming report issued by the United Nations Children's Fund.

Perhaps you consulted the Tyndall Report, which monitors evening network news, and wondered why some reports don't make the top ten list of news subjects on the networks during any month. Maybe you disagree and feel that your video is an important way of making sure the censored news gets to the public. Subscribing to a news clipping service or keeping news clippings on your own personal computer database helps to find subjects video worthy.

Perhaps you choose to monitor what's happening in the sparsely-populated desert areas, finding that the military has quietly resumed biowarfare testing. For example on January 27, 1973, the Salt Lake Tribune reported such headlines as: "Army Resumes Biological Agent Test ad Dugway (Utah) After 10-Year Cessation;" and "Dugway to test disease-causing agents at remote lab" (Author: Jim Woolf). There were the headlines of September 21, 1993, "Dugway Base Cited for 22 Waste Violations," (author: Laurie Sullivan). In the <u>High Country News</u>, the title appeared on September 8, 1993, "Biowarfare is Back," (author Jon Christensen). On September 15, 1993, the <u>High Desert Advocate</u> ran an article with the title, "Utah biowarfare oversight group wants to do its work behind closed doors."

If you kept news clippings of what was happening then in Dugway, Utah, you could have found funds from one of the video investigative reporting support groups, perhaps, or used your own low-budget to travel to the high desert area of Dugway, Utah with your video camera and talked to the people interested or involved in the matter.

Your investigative news angle would be: the U.S. Army has brought biological warfare testing back to the Dugway Proving Ground in the same western Utah location that ten years ago it claimed was not safe. The news angle is that military scientists are testing "the Biological Integrated Detection System" at the same facility the military says is now renovated. Is it? Your video would tell the news from an investigative reporting point of view, designed to expose corruption, if any exists, by interviewing experts and scientists.

The defensive weapon is supposed to detect the presence of biological agents. Your video would be about whether it works—whether it gives soldiers enough time to put on biohazard suits. The tests involved anthrax, botulism, and the plague.

To make your video, for an example, you'd have to interview Dugway representatives who would let you know in what liquid the germs were carried because the people of the town were afraid of the germs getting into the air. Doing some local history, you'd find out that the Dugway facility first closed in 1983 because of a fear that if there was an air leak in the sealed chamber, deadly germs would get into the air.

As your video progressed, you'd be able to show the viewers in exactly what ways the facility was renovated, and whether the safety precautions that exist now are enough to prevent a leak. Only experts and scientists interviewed on the video, and an up-close shot on the safety measure, could convince the public that safety was really that secure. Or is it? Would the military let you tape the renovation changes?

This is how you make your investigative videos of the news that normally doesn't get into the big city papers. An excellent resource of the stories that could make great videos can be found in the book, <u>Censored</u>, The News That Didn't Make the News and Why, Carl Jensen & Project Censored, published in 1994 by Four Walls Eight Windows, 39 West 14th St., #503, New York, NY 10011.

This excellent book contains chapters on raking muck and raising hell, U.S. censorship, and a lot of censored news that never made the news but should have. These include the biohazard story, and other news that would make excellent muckraking videos.

You even can send Project Censored interesting news you spot hidden in the back pages of your newspaper. Send your clippings to: Nomination, Project Censored, Sonoma State University, Rohnert Park, CA 94928. Their annual deadline is October 15th.

To make muckraking videos, you'll have to look in small-circulation magazines and or small-town rural newspapers as well as in your local big-city news, if you live in the big town. What you're looking for are stories you think should have received more coverage. Your video's purpose is to give those stories the coverage they deserve.

The video you make will be designed to show the public what's happening and why. The story should be timely and of national or global importance. If the story is significant, it's worthy of being made into a videocassette that you can offer to a variety of audiences, including the big-time media as well as the locals.

Stories you put on tape need not have appeared in the news. It could have appeared in a trade journal. Or it could have come from a local paper, or even a tabloid—if it's factual. It could have briefly been covered on television or overheard in a radio talk show interview.

Once you have written permission from where ever you saw it first to dig deeper into the story, find out whether it received any follow-up. If the lack of exposure is bothering the people in the news, offer to interview them on tape. Then dig deeper and interview others.

Get shots of where it happened, and ask the usual, what, who, when, where, how, and why questions. Show rather than tell on the tape. Avoid "talking head" shots that go on for minutes. Instead, cut to other scenes and do voice-overs to show movement and action.

What you're selling in this kind of video is simply the censored news, the news that most newspapers and magazines refuse to print. You're satisfying the public's right to know and make beneficial changes.

TARGET MARKET:

Muckraking videos that emphasize the news stories that the media usually censors primarily appeal to mail-order catalog customers. You can offer your video, if it fits the 23 or 53 minute news slots, to half-hour or full-hour news programs, or to producers of specials on network television.

Your advertising usually will be in specialty magazines that appeal to readers interested in a particular subject related to your expose video. You can offer your video to nonprofit organizations related to the subject of your tape, to the government, and to schools. Or you can give seminars on the subject of your expose and sell your tape at conventions or through bookstores, club meetings, and correspondence courses.

RELATED VIDEO OPPORTUNITIES:

Expose hoaxes on video. Making videos that expose corruption is related to alternative media public relations. Any government can hire a videographer to make a propaganda film or video. The question is on whose side are you on? Pick an industry you want to expose. Medicine? Meat packing? The funeral industry? Ecological disasters related to environmental terrorists? Cover-ups?

Related video opportunities exist with the alternative broadcast media producers and organizations. Look at the variety of video direct mail order catalogs.

You can make a social issues expose video of the self-enhancement industry. Find out what corruption hasn't been exposed yet.

Your goal is to empower the public. Show your readers or viewers why experts can be trusted. Have these experts offer solutions to common ground problems.

Expose government cover-ups with air-tight cases that even the tightest skeptics can't disprove. Have facts that can be checked and validated by experts and scientists who have reputations for being credible. Viewers will pay what they can afford to see information they can use to make important decisions—information that may never air on the network news.

ADDITIONAL INFORMATION:

Media Network
(clearinghouse for information

on social issue videotapes and films)
39 W. 14th St., suite 403
New York, NY 10011

8MM NEWS COLLECTIVE
c/o Squeaky Wheel
372 Connecticut Street
Buffalo, NY 14213

ALTERNATIVE RADIO
2129 Mapleton
Boulder, CO 80304

ALTERNATIVE NEWS
Box 7297
Austin, TX 78713

AMERICA'S DEFENSE MONITOR
1500 Massachusetts Ave., NW
Washington, DC 20005

BLACK PLANET PRODUCTIONS/
NOT CHANNEL ZERO
P.O. Box 435, Cooper Station
New York, NY 10003-O435

CALIFORNIA NEWSREEL
149 9th Street, Suite 420
San Francisco, CA 94103

COMMON GROUND
Stanley Foundation
216 Svcamore Street, Suite 500
Muscatine, IA 52761

DIVA-TV
c/o ACT-UP

135 W. 29th Street, #10
New York, NY 10001

EARTH COMMUNICATIONS
(Radio For Peace International)
Box 10869
Eugene, OR 97440

EL SALVADOR MEDIA PROJECT
335 W. 38th Street, 5th Fl.
New York, NY 10018

EMPOWERMENT PROJECT
3403 Highwav 54 West
Chapel Hill, NC 27516

ENVROVIDEOS
P.O. Box 629000
El Dorado Hills, CA 95762

GLOBALVISION
1600 Broadway
New York, NY 10019

THE INDEPENDENT
Association of Independent Video and Film
625 Broadway 9th fl.
New York, NY 10012

LABOR BEAT
37 S. Ashland Avenue
Chicago, IL 60607

MEDIA DEMOCRACY PROJECT
c/o Made in USA Productions
330 W. 42nd Street, Suite 1905
New York, NY 10036

MEDIA NETWORK/ ALTERNATIVE MEDIA INFORMATION CENTER
39 W. 14th Street, #403
New York, NY 10011

NATIONAL ASIAN AMERICAN TELECOMMUNICATIONS ASSOCIA-
TION
346 9th Street, 2nd Fl.
San Francisco, CA 94103

NATIONAL FEDERATION OF COMMUNITY BROADCASTERS
66611th Street NW, Suite 805
Washington, DC 2OOOl

PACIFICA NETWORK NEWS
702 H Street NW, Suite 3
Washington, DC 2OOO1

PACIFICA RADIO ARCHIVE
3729 Cahuenga Blvd., West
North Hollywood, CA 91604

PAPER TIGER TV/DEEP DISH
339 Lafayette Street
New York, NY 1OO12

P.O.V. (Points Of View)
330 W. 19th Street, 11th Fl.
New York, NY 10019

SECOND OPINION
Erwin Knoll (Host)
c/o The Progressive
409 E. Maln Stree
Madison, WI 53703

UNDERCURRENTS
130 W. 25th Street
New York, NY 10001

VIDEO DATABANK
37 S. Wabash
Chicago, IL 60603

THE VIDEO PROJECT:
FILMS AND VIDEOS FOR A SAFE AND SUSTAINABLE WORLD
5332 College Avenue, Suite 101
Oakland, CA 94618

41

Lowering the Costs of Foods and Groceries

What do you think it costs per month for nutritious, healthy food to feed one person, and what do you think it costs per month for food for a family of four? To find out look at **Dr. Matt's Guide to Nutritious Survival Foods** Web site at: http://www.mysteriesofthemind.com/dr-matt.htm. Interestingly, the Web site advises, "Get a high quality sprouter, Sonic Bloom, and a decent cache of seeds. That will be your best bet for long-term survival if everything goes to the toilet."

What I found helpful on the site is the table noting the cost of buying nutritious and healthy foods for a family or for an individual. What's helpful about the site is that it states, "There are two costs listed for every food item. The first is cost per ounce, which will usually be listed in the upper left-hand corner of the tag on the grocery shelf."

Note that the detail of the Web site is very important to making a budget or plan. A short excerpt reads, "The first is cost per ounce, which will usually be listed in the upper left-hand corner of the tag on the grocery shelf."

According to *Dr. Matt's Guide to Nutritious Survival Foods* Web site, "buying larger cans is not always cheaper." The site lists the most relevant cost that you won't find easily elsewhere. It's the cost per hundred calories. In your budget and plan, list the calories you want to eat per meal. Then look up the most important information, which is the cost per hundred calories.

This information is what you need to develop your budget. So look at the tables on the Web site and decide whether the Web site's "Sample 30-day 'Bare-Bones' Grocery List for a Single Person" is what you need. With a little more than 20 dollars each week, the 30-day grand total grocery list for one person sums up to only **$82.64.** Then look at the site's "Sample 90-Day Grocery List for a Family of Four." The Web site's sample 90-day grocery list grand total adds up to **$1421.19.**

How do these figures fit in your budget and plan for food expenses? Bookmark the Web site and study those totals. Compare them to your actual expenses and read Dr. Matt's excellent advice. How do your food expenses compare?

Note that food costs change with each passing year. Print out Dr. Matt's Guide to Nutritious Survival Foods and put it in a place where you'll see it daily, like on the side of your refrigerator and in the file where you keep your monthly food expenses budget. *Dr. Matt's Guide to Nutritious Survival Foods* contains recent food prices. The copyright year is 2004. Compare the prices you pay for your food with the cost of the foods listed in the guide.

Are you eating healthy, nutritious foods? How do survival foods compare with comfort foods? Are the same? Should they be? Do you grow your own vegetables? What's your soil like? Is it free from toxic wastes such as decades-old dumped rocket fuel or other poisons? Think about how much you will spend on food costs. What type of budget and food list, guide, or table can give you more choices? Now make a budget listing other expenses of living. What's the most important and powerful lesson you've learned from living?

Index

0-595-34772-X

www.ingramcontent.com/pod-product-compliance
Lightning Source LLC
Chambersburg PA
CBHW030933180526
45163CB00002B/554